Nick:

A Young Hero Remembered

Erin Hulshizer

PublishAmerica
Baltimore

© 2005 by Erin Hulshizer.
All rights reserved. No part of this book may be reproduced, stored in a retrieval system or transmitted in any form or by any means without the prior written permission of the publishers, except by a reviewer who may quote brief passages in a review to be printed in a newspaper, magazine or journal.

First printing

At the specific preference of the author, PublishAmerica allowed this work to remain exactly as the author intended, verbatim, without editorial input.

ISBN: 1-4241-0048-8
PUBLISHED BY PUBLISHAMERICA, LLLP
www.publishamerica.com
Baltimore

Printed in the United States of America

Dedication

This book is dedicated to our son, Nicholas, and to all of those who believe in the power of faith and hope.

Acknowledgments

I wish to express sincere gratitude to my family and friends whose support and encouragement were deeply appreciated. I am particularly grateful to Joan Boyd, who not only believed in my story, but who also helped me see it through to publication.

Chapter 1

From the time I was small, I wanted one thing out of life, and that was to be a mother. When other kids were dreaming of the spectacular careers that they would have one day, I was in the house "playing house." I begged my parents to have another baby, insuring them that they wouldn't have to lift a finger in the child's upbringing. When they didn't fall for my pleading, I did the best I could with the resources available to me. I cut babies out of the JC Penney's catalogue. I arranged the infants on my bedroom floor, turned off the lights, left the room, and waited for them to come to life. Peeking around the corner, I'd watch for movement. Once caught, of course, the babies would remain real and then I would take care of them. At least that's what I wanted to happen, but sadly, my plan failed.

In 1992, I graduated from Iowa State University with a degree in elementary education. That same summer I married my best friend and got my first job as a preschool teacher in Ames. Shortly before our first wedding anniversary, Doug gave in to my persuading and we were soon awaiting the birth of our first child, Allison.

Being a mother was nothing like I had imagined. No one could have prepared me for the exhaustion of late night feedings, around-the-clock responsibility, and the worry involved in being a parent. Despite all of that, however, I found myself reveling in the overwhelming love and tenderness between mother and child.

By January of 1997, Allison lost her status as "only child" with the arrival of our second daughter Kate. Overnight life went from busy to chaotic as we adjusted to taking care of a jealous toddler and a needy newborn. Late at night, however, with the rest of my family soundly sleeping, I was able to reflect on all of the many blessings that had been bestowed upon Doug and me. I thought of that little girl who had dreamed, not so long ago, of motherhood, and then in the blink of an eye, who had achieved that dream. As I faded into an exhaustion induced coma on the couch, I thanked God for allowing me the privilege of parenthood and, thereby, the immense happiness found.

By the time Kate turned eighteen months old, I was starting to feel the familiar desire to have another baby. Doug and I were again faced with the dilemma of whether or not to have more children. Discussions ensued and lists of pros and cons were considered. In the end, weighing all factors against my desire to have another baby, we came to the conclusion that it would be in our best interest not to have any more children. So, it came as something of a surprise when I discovered that I was expecting again.

It was my birthday and my mom and dad had come for a visit. As was our custom, we gave our visiting parents our bed. The sofa bed, needing to be destroyed, and the girls' bunk beds, which squeaked so badly made it virtually impossible to sleep. We felt guilty offering our parents either one. So, this night, Doug and I opted for the bunk beds. If I remember correctly, we got the giggles thinking that with any move we made Mom and Dad would probably think we were up to something... which, as it turned out, gave us the idea to be up to something. Not prepared for "something," our encounter was not entirely without risk. As it turned out, I was to get my heart's secret desire and Doug, well, he got used to the idea after a little while.

My pregnancy progressed, and by the seventh week, morning sickness had made its presence known. I wasn't physically ill, thank goodness, but sometimes I think I would have felt better if I could have been. My sense of smell was working against me, and I remember being completely nauseated by the smell of the Christmas decorations. Do Christmas decorations have a smell one might ask? Yes! They do!
At eighteen weeks, we had our first ultrasound. Doug and I had already discussed ahead of time whether or not we should find out the sex of our baby. We decided since we had found out with the girls, it would be fun to wait until delivery with this one. When the ultrasound technician said that she could see the sex of the baby, did we want to know, we very dutifully said no, that we would wait and be surprised. I truly doubted my own resolve on this matter, but since Doug and I were in this

together, I thought that I would be able to restrain myself for his sake. That was, until the nurse happened to say "he" once when referring to our baby during the ultrasound. The second we left the exam room, I turned to Doug and said "Did you hear her say 'he'?" Had she said that to throw us off track? Did she refer to all babies as 'he'? My resolve completely destroyed, Doug and I made our way home, videotape in hand. We spent an hour or more that night scrutinizing our video; pausing, rewinding, and then fast-forwarding again. "Did you see that?" Rewind and pause. "There!" We were having a boy. On my next doctor visit, when I asked, our theory was confirmed. We were going to have a son.

Our son was a beautiful baby from the start. His ultrasound pictures graced our refrigerator, proudly displayed next to current pictures of his sisters. We made phone calls to family members, who were excited for us to be adding a male member to the family tree. All in all, I had never been happier in my life. I had a wonderful husband, two beautiful little girls, and now a son to make our family complete.

Each month as my abdomen continued to protrude I had Doug take my picture. I would hold my fingers up to indicate which month of pregnancy I was currently in, something I had always meant to do when expecting the girls, but had never done. Our son's baby book would begin with photos taken before he had even taken his first breath.

My advanced pregnancy was not entirely without concern. Several months before our baby was to be born, I was already measuring at full term. Tests were inconclusive. We knew there was only one baby and, although the amniotic fluid was a little excessive, it was not enough to account for the size of my uterus. To be sure there wasn't anything to be concerned about, my doctor kept me under close supervision. I went in weekly for non-stress tests to be sure the baby wasn't showing signs of distress. I think these tests proved more to be more a sign of my distress because in my thirty-third week of pregnancy, the monitor showed that I was having contractions every three minutes.

An exam indicated that I was beginning to dilate, and so, my doctor did what he thought was necessary and admitted me into the hospital as a precaution against preterm labor. I was given medication to stop contractions and was injected with steroid shots to speed up development of the baby's lungs in the event that his birth was imminent. Suffering from doctor anxiety and fainting twice on a hospital floor, the thought of being admitted to the hospital terrified me. So that afternoon, watching Doug and the girls leave, I was scared to death. I wasn't overly concerned about the baby coming because of all the steps that had been taken to prevent further labor. I just really wanted to go home with my family. The next morning, after further monitoring showed that my contractions had subsided, I was sent home. I was given some pills to take daily which would keep me from having premature contractions.

When I reached my thirty-sixth week of pregnancy, I was instructed to stop taking the pills. I was more than ready to quit the medication by that time because of their unpleasant side effects, most significant of which was uncontrollable shakiness. My last pill taken, I proceeded to go about my normal activities until about 1:30 PM the following afternoon when my water broke.

Doug and I had decided, after my night in the hospital, to rent a pager so I could get hold of him no matter where he was. When I couldn't reach him at work, I called his pager. He would tell me later that he had been at a meeting at a local restaurant and that when the pager buzzed him, he and his colleagues jumped out of their skin. He said his boss threw him the keys to the company pick-up out in the parking lot and told him to go. Once back at his office to pick up his own car, Doug called and I filled him in on the pertinent details: water broke, no contractions yet, but get home quick! Then I called my dad on his cell phone and told him what was going on. What is it about "Mom and Dad" that enables you to cry when you're nervous and scared? I had remained calm, cool, and collected until I heard my dad's voice. But once I heard his very distinctive 'hello' as he answered his phone, tears welled up in my eyes and my voice started shaking. As Dad could do, he made me feel better and assured me that they would come as soon as they could.

My side informed, I called Doug's parents. Both retired, they had graciously offered to come down and stay with Allison and Kate when the baby came. They would leave within the hour, but had a two-hour drive ahead of them. I called our good friends, Wayne and Jana, and they offered to watch the girls while Jay and Marlene were en route.

My bag was packed; the girls' bag was packed; directions for Jay and Marlene on the girls' whereabouts were left on the kitchen counter. I was inspecting the fridge and freezer for meal possibilities for everyone when Doug came through the door. He had that expectant, half worried, and half excited look on his face, like perhaps the 75 mph he had driven to get home might not have been quick enough.

Fortunately, or unfortunately, things weren't going to be moving that fast. The girls dropped off, Doug and I drove to the clinic to confirm that my water had, in fact, broken. I didn't need anyone to tell me that as I'd been sitting in wet pants for the past hour. The doctor admitted me to the hospital, because even though I was not in active labor, there could be an increased chance of infection since my water had broken. The news we were given was not particularly encouraging. Because the baby would be considered preterm if born right now, they would not induce labor until the chance of infection outweighed the benefits of leaving the baby in the womb. What this meant for us is that we would sit in the hospital, me in wet pants, for up to three days. If I did not go into labor on my own by then, at that point I would be induced. Having been introduced to Pitocin once before, I knew it was not an experience I wanted to repeat.

Mercifully, around 5:30AM the next morning, I was awakened by the familiar "pop" that I had come to know meant that active labor had just begun for me. I have asked my doctor since then what that "pop" is and he couldn't say. I compare it to a balloon popping, but since I've always been awakened from a deep sleep by it, I'm never sure if I hear it or feel it. Sure enough, contractions began and very quickly escalated to the "okay, this isn't fun" stage. An exam at around 7:30 showed that I had dilated to 4cm, and my doctor said that around 1:00 or 2:00 we should have a baby. Experiencing considerable pain, I thought that was a heck of a long time.

The nurse came in as the doctor left and we began

discussing pain medications. My contractions were very strong and painful by now and any thought of trying to go without drugs was quickly going out the window. As she was turning to leave, I was really feeling the need to have a BM. I told her this and in the next instant she was a white blur as she spun out the door. Did having a BM require special equipment when one is in active labor, or did she just not wish to be there when nature took its course? "Hey, my shift is almost over, the next nurse can help you out. See ya!" As I was wondering what I had said wrong, in rushed the doctor pulling on rubber gloves at the same time that my nurse was trying to help him into his surgical gown. Upon further examination it was confirmed that I was fully dilated and ready to start pushing. It had been less than 30 minutes since the last exam and now, my having no drugs and my doctor in red high tops, our son was ready to be born.

On June 17, 1999 at 8:40 AM, Nicholas Drew Hulshizer was born. We had chosen the middle name of Drew because it had as many letters in it as possible to represent the men in our families: Douglas for Doug, Robert for my mom's side, Edward for my dad's side and Wayne for Doug's dad's side. At 6 pounds 5 ounces and 18 1/2 inches long, Nicholas was as healthy and as perfect as he could be despite his early entrance into this world. As with the girls, the love and pride Doug and I felt when we looked at our son's tiny little face for the first time was indescribable. It was after that day that I began to pray a prayer that I would pray every day from that day forth: "Dear God, thank you so much for all that we have been given. Guide us and watch over us. We pray that you will protect us from harm, illness, and violence. We have been given so much already that I have nothing more that I need. I can only ask that we not lose what we already have. Amen."

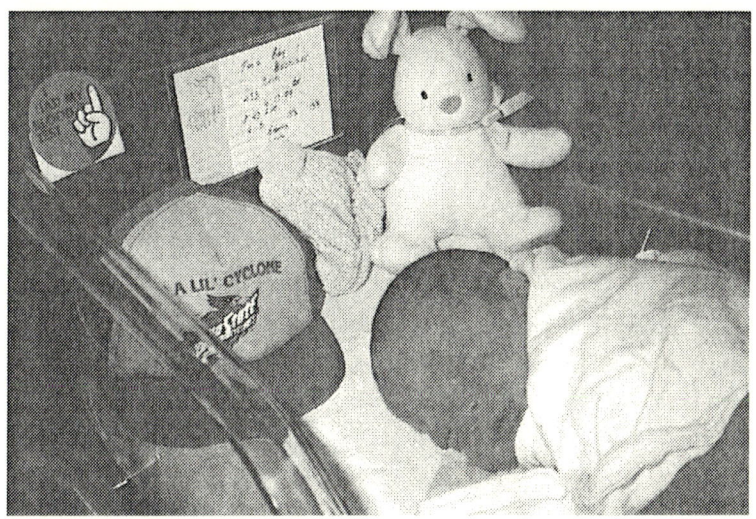

Later that day, Grandpa and Grandma Hulshizer brought the big sisters to see their new brother. I remember my shock at Kate's appearance as she walked through the door. She had on one of her favorite shorts outfits. It was a one-piece deal and had big orange and yellow flowers all over it. There were three buttons down the front and a big white collar embroidered with flower leaves. A cute outfit, to be sure, when it is worn facing the right direction. To complete the ensemble, Kate was sporting her black, patent leather church shoes, without socks. At two-and-a-half I was reasonably certain that she had insisted on looking this way, but I thought it best not to say anything "just in case." Allison, on the other hand, was wearing her favorite dark purple, flannel dress with her white summer sandals. Seems the two were confused as to what season we were currently in, so chose to represent both. When confused as to what to do, cover all your bases. Why I remember certain details such as how our daughters were dressed, I do not know. But what I do know is that that day is full of special memories and I am thankful for them all.

Grandpa Jay, Grandma Marlene, Allie and Kate all took turns holding Nicholas while Doug and I worked really hard to stay awake and enjoy the whole thing. The girls were thrilled to be big sisters, but I could see a little bit of hesitance in their faces at all the attention the baby was getting; the "What am I, chopped liver?" routine.

Eventually, Grandpa and Grandma took the girls home, and Doug and I did our best to get some rest between visits from friends, phone calls and nurses popping in every few minutes. Despite the wonderful care and pampering I was receiving, I couldn't wait to take our baby home and have our whole family all together at last.

The day after Nicholas was born, June 18, my mom and dad arrived. They did the tag team thing with Jay and Marlene, taking over care of the girls until Doug and I got to come home. Again the girls arrived to visit us, this time accompanied by Grandpa Jon and Grandma Dianne. Now they were wearing matching t-shirts that read: "I'm the big sister" and "I'm in the middle." They stood there patiently and proudly so we could take pictures of them in their shirts and holding the baby. One day we could show them just how darling they looked and how excited they were to have a baby brother. These are the pictures a mother plans on saving to pull out some day when the sisters have their brother sitting out on a corner with a "For Sale" sign taped to his back. "Look at these pictures, girls. See how sweet and loving you were? You love your brother, honest, you do!"

Nick came home and the days that followed were wonderful, if not exhausting. Nicholas was absorbed into our lives with enthusiasm. The girls loved to hold their baby brother and were invaluable as helpers. Doug couldn't wait to come home from work each night to play with his brood, and I was the happiest person in the world.

Nicholas proved to be one of those babies causing me to think, "Man, I could have ten of these!" He was easygoing and content to just take things in. That didn't mean that he didn't present us with a hurdle now and then, such as sleeping at night. He was of the opinion that if he took the trouble to wake up, then he should be given something in return. The something that he felt he wanted was me, in the form of a human pacifier. So, I did what any sleep deprived mother would do and I moved myself into his room. I had it down to a system. The moment I felt my little bunkie stir, I could begin to nurse him. The most important thing I had learned was not to let the baby completely wake up, otherwise I could count on being up for at least an hour. Through my method, I could have Nicholas counting Z's in ten minutes or so. Any baby book will recommend not sleeping with the baby. It is a bad idea for any number of reasons, but it worked well for me, and those are memories I will always treasure.

As the days and weeks passed, Nick continued to be very mellow. When other babies were rolling over and crawling, he wasn't. He was a charming little guy and knew that all he had to do was flash that smile of his and anything he desired would be laid at his feet or put in his mouth. It is amazing the communication that exists between a baby and his caregivers. Nary a word has to be uttered, and the baby is able to make his needs known. Nick was good at this and quickly became the prince of our household. He beckoned and we rushed to be of service.

The day finally came when Nick decided he was ready to expand his horizons and become mobile. He again did it in traditional Nick style, slow and easy. He didn't crawl like other babies. He had developed his own very unique method, and I'm not even sure how to describe it. Picture how a regular baby crawls on all fours. Okay, it was nothing like that. He would sit, and then extend one leg forward along with the corresponding arm. Then he would scoot himself forward on his tush. I have actually, on several occasions, tried to recreate this movement, but quite frankly have never been successful. It worked for Nick, however; and as one hand was basically free, he was capable of toting things along with him.

By this point, Nick did have a favorite possession. It was the little item that, when left behind, we were obliged to immediately turn around and go back to get it. The girls never did have a favorite thing, but Nick had his "burpie." Nick's burpie is what some might call a burp rag or a cloth diaper. I had gotten in the habit of putting a burpie in his crib with him, something to snuggle with, but not something he could get tangled up in or chew the eye off. The day I peeked in at him sleeping soundly in his crib with a huge portion of his burpie stuffed securely in his mouth was the day that Nick and Burpie became inseparable. Now that Nick was on the move, Burpie was usually along for the ride.

By the time Nick was about eighteen months old, he decided he'd had enough of just sitting back and taking everything in. He became a master fit thrower when something wasn't going his way. I mean the kind where the child throws himself to the floor and thrashes around kicking and screaming. It really shouldn't have been funny and it wasn't when it occurred someplace like church, but here was Mr. Calm, Cool and Collected, just realizing that things weren't always going to go his way, and darn it, he wasn't going to sit back and just take that lightly!

The girls found his fits hilarious and were tempted now and then to invoke one. I think that was the plan the first day that they did Nick's hair up in bows and a headband, which in itself, was quite impressive given that Nick had very little hair to work with. But their plan backfired when Nick came out of the bathroom patting his blond little head and saying, "pretty!" He was very proud of his appearance, and Allie and Kate decided, after some thought, that this just might be funnier than watching one of his fits. Whenever the girls were in the bathroom getting "pretty," Nick was generally right there with them.

Despite the feminine influence in his life, Nick was Daddy's little buddy through and through and they both knew it. The moment Nick heard the garage door open when Doug came home at the end of the day, he would go racing for the door. "Daddy!" From the moment the door opened until we sat down for supper, Nick was attached to Daddy's arm with no hope for removal.

Daddy was the fun one. While I had some much needed time to myself (doing dishes), Doug would wrestle with the kids, give them various animal rides around the house, tickle them, tease them and dance with them. Daddy even made clean-up time fun. He'd invent some sort of a game and the next thing they knew, the unpleasant task the girls were griping about doing was done, with laughter no less!

But work or play, if Daddy was home, Nick was usually with him. If they weren't inside playing, they were outside swinging on the tire swing, riding the tractor, or picking up sticks for the fire pit. If there was a fix-it job to be done, Nick was the tool holder, and a darn good one at that. Basically, where there was one there was the other.

On the other hand, my designated responsibilities were book reader, ouwie kisser, and tushie cleaner. Nick wasn't showing a whole lot of interest in the potty seat, but knew enough to tap his diaper suggestively and tell me "poo-poo." These words, once uttered, usually meant the race was on. The moment I indicated that a diaper change was in store, Nick was off and running, giggling the whole way. Once caught, I'd scoop him up for a zerbert on the tummy, only to be reminded why we were heading for a diaper change in the first place. "P.U.! Do you have a skunk tush?!"

"No." Huge grin.

Bath time was not one of my more favorite times with the children, probably the reason they got by with as few baths as possible. Baths were too much fun. Translated, way too much fun meant way too much water over way too much of the bathroom. The girls also had a problem with the fact that Nick always whizzed the moment his feet touched water. This completely grossed them out, but I soon learned that if they didn't see him pee, they were okay. Put Nick in the tub before the girls arrived and "voila!" no pee in the water. A number two in the water was not so easy to camouflage, however, and bath time generally ended there on the spot, soaped or not.

If bath time was one of my least favorite times, bedtime was one of my favorites. The girls in their jammies, teeth brushed and freshly pottied, we'd sit on their bedroom floor and read books. Whoever picked the book to be read would sit on my lap and the other would snuggle by my side. Then we'd switch. Doug was usually getting Nick ready for bed at this time, but occasionally Nick would come in and read books with we girls. This rarely went over well, because Nick insisted on being on my lap despite who was the legal lap sitter at the time. I would promise the offended party an extra book the next night and we were back in business with Prince Nick in the driver's seat.

Always after books came prayers. My three babies would lay in bed with their hands folded and praying "Now I lay me down to sleep." Even Nick, by two years of age, was saying this prayer with Doug and me every night. All three knew the importance of praying and they were as proud of themselves as we were of them for saying them. Then, as my parents did with me, I'd kiss them good-night and blow out the light. Despite how chaotic the day had been, I always felt a little hesitant closing their doors for the night. If I close the door, will they still be there in the morning? Or has this all just been a wonderful dream?

Nicholas turned two years old in our "new" house. I use the term "new" loosely, because the house we moved into was built in 1900. It was, however, a new house to us. Doug and I had always wanted to have an acreage in the country, and when this one came up and we could afford it, we jumped at the chance. We were to find out later, why the house was so cheap, mainly because we hadn't yet paid for all of the things that would make the house livable. Like a working septic system and outlets that didn't shoot flames.

Anyway, despite these little glitches, we had many good times in our house. I always liked the mornings. Not the getting up part, but the general laziness of them. As I mentioned, I stayed home with our children. This allowed me the luxury of being able to sleep in until about fifteen minutes before Allie needed to get on the school bus. Doug always got her up and saw that she was fed and dressed, but my duty was hair. Not that he wasn't capable of a mean "do" himself, I think it had more to do with a "guys don't do hair" attitude.

So, my mornings usually went something like this: My alarm would go off at 6:30. That was just to make it appear that I had intentions of getting up that early. Then I would press snooze until 7:00 at which time I was usually wide awake. I wasn't ready to get up, however, because I still had fifteen minutes left until hair time. There is something so delicious about lying in bed, all snug and warm with the sun just beginning to rise outside the bedroom window. No one is fighting, screaming or whining. There isn't anything needing my immediate attention, and I can pretend for just a moment that life is really peaceful and serene.

That is, until I see a little blond head bobbing above the level of my blankets. There's the familiar crinkling sound of diaper and then the unmistakable tugging of the sheets as the perpetrator pulls himself atop the bed. I close my eyes quickly so as to appear to be asleep. I can feel him crawling closer. A knee comes down hard upon a tender part of my anatomy, and yet I don't flinch. I'm a pro, but nothing can help me when my little bed buddy begins "the stare." He's been told repeatedly not to wake Mommy up, so he doesn't utter a word, he just stares at my closed eyes, willing them to open. My eyes are closed tightly, but his will is strong. I can hold out no longer, and I give Nick my first smile for the day. "Morning, Buddy."

"Hi, Mommy." It was going to be a good day.

Doug left the house just a few minutes before Allie's bus came at 7:30. Kate, Nick and I, just out of bed and still in our jammies, were ready to start our day as well. First order of business was what to have for breakfast. Anyone who knows me knows what a tremendous chocoholic I am. Our breakfast menu usually consisted of the following choices: chocolate cereal, chocolate Pop-tarts, chocolate muffins, or chocolate peanut butter on toast. There was a time when I felt a little guilty about allowing my children to eat like I did, but then some very bright fellow somewhere did some tests and discovered that apparently and luckily chocolate has some very redeeming qualities. I don't feel quite so bad anymore.

Although given the breakfast items from which to choose, every morning Nick had to check to be sure I hadn't added candy and freeze pops to the list. I wish I could bottle the look that he gave me when asking for "Tandy, pease." That would be some pretty powerful stuff! He'd stand there looking up at me with those big blue eyes, total and complete sweetness. And note the manners. I'd counteroffer with a chocolate Pop-tart and a promise of candy after lunch. His response was, "no ah too, Mommy" (translation: "No thank you, Mommy"). This was said with a hand held up and a shake of the head. "Feeze pop pease, Mommy?" The boy knew I was weakening, but I could see Kate watching me from the table and I knew she was waiting to see if I'd give in.

I admit, regrettably, to treating each of the children with varying degrees of strictness. Allison, bless her heart, had been our guinea pig. With her, we knew how we should be raising her, by the book, so to speak, but then Kate came along and we had relaxed some. We were realizing that she wouldn't be ruined if we let things slide here and there. "You want to wear your tu-tu to Wal-Mart? Fine, just get your shoes on!" With Nick I was considering letting him have a freeze pop for breakfast. He was just so gosh darn cute! But the mother in me persevered and I sat Nick down to the table with a chocolate Pop-tart and a sippy cup filled with chocolate milk.

I take this opportunity to defend myself lest I be thought a nutritional failure for my children. My children are given fruits and vegetables and all that good stuff. Chocolate is just really, really good at breakfast.

After we made it through breakfast, I would try my best to get Kate and Nick involved in an activity that would buy me time for a shower. Play-dough and paints worked very well, but if I really wanted to please them,

I'd dig out the tea set from the toy kitchen and let them have a tea party. Kool-aid for tea and marshmallows for sugar cubes. Kate would pour and they would both drink out of the fancy little pink cups. Kate and Nick had their typical brother and sister moments, but they were also the best of friends. Kate catered to Nick's every whim and Nick worshipped the ground she walked on.

The rest of our day was pretty much the same as the day before. Kate and Nick would play while I did my household chores. They'd play house, which I always got a big kick out of. Kate, dressed in some get-up from the dress-up box, would be setting the table for the fabulous meal she had prepared. Then I'd hear Nick calling "Haaahneey." Doug and I call one another "Honey," so here was Nick, absorbed in his role as husband, calling his make-believe wife "Honey." Precious.

After a well-balanced and nutritious lunch, we'd go outside and play. Nick loved to go outside. Throughout the morning he had already asked me several times "Go ouside, Mommy?" He'd be standing there holding his black play shoes and be pointing towards the door. Now that it was time to go out, he could hardly stand his excitement. Prepared for what was in store, I grabbed a lawn chair and followed him to the swing-set. Once in his little yellow swing with the bar pulled down, Nick was a happy guy. He would stay in that swing until my legs and arms gave out from pushing, hence the chair. Still, the time came when the swinging had to stop. At that point Kate did a pretty good job of persuading him into another activity. They both enjoyed the sandbox, although as sand will do, it made its way into some pretty remote places. I much preferred digging in the dirt myself. At least I knew what to expect when clean-up time came.

Eventually, naptime would roll around and it was time to go back inside. Bribery was called for at this time, and we would go in for a freeze pop. Hands and face somewhat cleaned up and freeze pop inhaled, I would get Kate situated with a movie and Nick and I would head to Mommy and Daddy's bed for a nap.

Since moving to this house, we had decided not to put the crib back up, and so Nick was given the girls' old bunk beds. He liked the big bed and slept very well, once he was asleep. It was getting him to stay in his bed long enough to fall asleep that was the problem. At bedtime, we'd read a book, say prayers, give kisses and then leave Nick to fall asleep on his own. That had been our routine since he was about a year old. For some reason, though, the newfound freedom of a bed with no bars proved to be a bit of a temptation. Doug and I would be sitting on the couch, all snuggled in, and we'd get the feeling of being watched. Sure enough, there would be Nick lying in the doorway between the den and the family room. He had apparently army crawled his way across the floor so as not to be detected. After repeatedly trying to return him to his bed, one of us would give in and go lay on the floor next to his bed. This was the squeaky bunk bed so we knew better than to actually lie in bed with him. It was hard enough escaping from the floor, let alone from a noisy bed.

Now that it was naptime, the same problem applied. I had discovered that lying down with him in our bed was mutually pleasant. Nick was, in fact, eager to take a nap if I would lie next to him. He would get his burpie and I would pull all the shades down. And finally, the piece de resistance, the fan. There are some people who laugh at us for sleeping with a fan on every night, but for a good, sound, peaceful sleep, there's nothing like the sound of a purring fan to get the job done.

The stage set, I lay Nick right smack dab in the center of the bed. The theory being that he wouldn't roll off should I remain awake and leave the bed before he did. I would lay on the little sliver of the bed that was left for me, and Nick would lay there sucking on his burpie, one hand always in contact with my arm. Naptime with Nick was a time I looked forward to every day, and it is a memory I will treasure for the rest of my life.

When Nick awoke from his nap, he'd emerge from the bedroom still sucking on his burpie. It generally wasn't a good idea to try to talk with him too much at this point, but a good snuggle would go pretty far. For the next twenty minutes or so, we'd sit and rock in the recliner, his head on my shoulder. He had the silkiest hair and I loved the feel of it against my cheek.

Usually, about this time, Allie would get home from school and Nick and Kate were ready for action again. After having been at school all day, Allie took a dim view to their attention, but with a snack in her belly and a cartoon or two, she'd come around and soon there'd be laughing and running (and fighting) in the house again.

Between 5:25 and 5:30 PM, Doug would get home from work. I can write these times so specifically, because he was always home by then. In fact, I would get slightly alarmed if he wasn't home by 5:35 which was late for him. His co-workers had commented to me several times about how Doug was always ready to go at the end of the day. Not because he didn't enjoy his job, but because he was anxious to get home to his family. I knew they were right, because all one had to do was watch him with his children to know how much they meant to him.

After the initial excitement of Daddy's coming home, we would both break off into our designated assignments. Mine was supper preparation and Doug's was controlling the troops. For me this meant peace and quiet in the kitchen, for Doug it meant an hour on the floor being pounced upon, and for the kids, it meant fun, pure and simple.

Each night, as the children all lay sleeping snug in their beds, and with the methodical sound of Doug's snoring in my ear, I again thought of how very fortunate I was. There wasn't one thing, of any importance anyway, that I would change in my life. I prayed my prayer again, thanking God for all we'd been given, asking for his guidance and protection, and asking that nothing bad happen to take away any of our current happiness.

Chapter 2

On September 21, 2001 at 5:45 PM we were in the driveway about to leave for Clinton, Iowa to visit my mom and dad. We were all excited to get away. We'd been up to our eyeballs in unpacking after our move in June and we were really looking forward to our first weekend away. I was also heading back to work on Monday. The job that I had at the middle school the previous year as an aide had become available again, and although I wasn't ready to go back to work, we really needed the money. Nick had just finished taking inventory, something he always did the moment we got in the car. "Oppie (burpie), Mommy?" Check! I handed Nick his burpie. "Juice, Mommy?" Check! I handed Nick his sippy cup. Once assured that these things were in fact along, he handed them back to me and I put them back in the diaper bag. I actually was thankful that Nick always checked for these things before we got too far from home, because on a couple of rare occasions, we had forgotten one or the other, and believe you me, it was not pretty. We'd be handing him anything resembling fabric, hoping there would be something he would suck on in the absence of Burpie. But, alas, Burpie was not to be replaced. Doug had earplugs in the car for just such an occasion, but the rest of us really suffered.

The girls in their car seats in the back with drinks, snacks, and toys at hand, and Nick in his car seat in the middle, our mini-van was loaded and ready for the three-hour trip to Grandpa and Grandma's house. We were actually very fortunate that our children rode wonderfully in the car. The younger two would sleep most of the way and Allie would quietly keep herself occupied.

Around 9:00 PM we pulled into the driveway. Everyone was awake and excited by now, and Dad was already coming out of the garage to greet us with his monster bear hugs that left us gasping for air. Mom would be in the kitchen baking and the fresh smell of Pine-sol would still be hanging in the air mingled with the aroma of several burning candles. Smelled like home.

My mom worked like 200 hours a week as a third grade teacher. Whenever company came she'd work up to the last minute trying to get the house cleaned and food prepared. I always told her not to bother with the house and food for just us. She'd say, "Oh, I won't. I just don't have time." But when it came down to it, she'd bust her behind to see that everything was prepared anyway.

Doug carried in all of our stuff from the van and I set about getting beds ready for the kids. The girls slept upstairs in the guest bedroom and Doug, Nick and I slept downstairs in the "audio-visual" room, not under any circumstances to be confused with a basement. This was Dad's domain, lovingly constructed to house all of his electronic equipment and his many assorted collections; Star Wars memorabilia, innumerable model motorcycles, antique radios, etc.

Up until this visit, Nick had always slept in Mom and Dad's old crib, but since he wasn't sleeping in a crib at home anymore, I told Mom I would just make him a bed on the couch next to the sofa bed where Doug and I slept. I had a cozy little nest made for him and put a bedrail under the sofa cushion so he wouldn't be able to roll out of his bed.

Given that it was already 9:45 PM, Mom and I got the girls to bed and then I took Nick downstairs to see if I could get him to sleep. It's not easy sleeping away from home for most people, and for Nick it was no exception. We had never gotten in the habit of rocking our children to sleep, and to do so now would further complicate an already disturbed routine. So, I got Nick snuggled into his make-shift bed with his burpie and one of his own blankets from home, then I sat in the recliner and waited for him to fall asleep. He lay there, not moving, but I could see his eyes were still open. After sitting there in the dark for 45 minutes, I thought I had better get up before I was down for the count myself. The room was dark except for the light from the fish tank, but try as I might, I wasn't quite able to make an exit without being noticed. I had almost made it to the steps when I heard "Mommy?"

"Nick, you need to go nigh nigh, okay?"

"Otay." He lay back down, but I could tell he was close to tears. He was so tired, but he didn't want to be alone. "You lie down and Mommy will be right back, okay?"

"Otay, Mommy."

I went upstairs, certain that he would fall asleep waiting for me to come back. But he didn't. Five minutes later we heard a creaking on the steps and Nick's tousled little head appeared from the lower level. He looked at us from a head lowered with guilt. He knew he wasn't supposed to be out of bed, but he also knew he wasn't going to stay down there all by himself. Doug and I looked at one another with the "what should we do" look. But there was Nick clutching his burpie with a look that begged not to be sent back to bed. So Doug did what I was hoping he would, and put his arms out to Nick. Nick fell asleep in his Daddy's arms that night. The last night that he was ours.

The next morning we had a leisurely breakfast with Mom, Dad, and all three of my grandparents. My Grandma Gill had been living with my parents for thirteen years and my Grandma and Grandpa Detwiler had recently moved to Clinton from Springfield, Missouri. Sitting there at the breakfast table all together brought back wonderful memories from my childhood when we would all drive many hours to be together for the holidays. Only this was no holiday, and already my children knew their great-grandparents better than I had known them myself at their age.

As after any meal there were dishes to be done and a kitchen to be cleaned, so like the "traditional" family, the women folk headed to the kitchen and the men folk headed outside with the kids. Mom and I visited while we did the dishes and looking out the window occasionally, we could see the kids riding bikes up and down the driveway. Bikes which had been rescued from a premature demise from someone else's trash pile by a loving grandpa. My dad could fix anything, and if one weren't overly concerned about cosmetics, his treasures were great.

Our chores concluded, Mom and I joined the others outside. They had finished with bikes and were in the backyard shooting arrows. Doug had set up an archery target and the kids were taking turn shooting the bow that he had made for Allie. Allie was a darn good little shot. She looked like a pro with her arm guard and her perfect form. Kate was being difficult, as Kate often was, and she'd decided she didn't want a turn. So now Doug was kneeling down behind Nick with his arms wrapped around Nick's body and guiding his tiny hands to their correct positions on the bow. Nick was so proud of himself, he could have burst. He was concentrating hard on what Daddy was telling him to do, and his excitement showed on his face. He was doing a big kid thing and he wasn't going to mess it up. Daddy and Nick pulled back the string together and when they let go, the arrow went sailing toward the target. The arrow bounced off the center and landed on the ground, but by the expression on Nick's face one would have thought he had just made the most difficult of shots. We all clapped and Nick beamed with pride.

Because the day was quickly getting away from us, we planned our itinerary for the rest of the day. We would pack a picnic and drive to Maquoketa, Iowa, where we planned to have a picnic lunch at the Hurstville Lime Kilns after which we would browse through some local antique stores.

The drive up was nice and once in Maquoketa, Dad drove by the family home of his biological mother. A mother whom we had found fifty some years after his birth and whom we have since come to know and love. An ironic story actually, that my dad should be transferred from St. Louis, Missouri to within miles of his place of birth in Iowa.

Nick was sound asleep by the time we stopped for our picnic. We left him sleeping in the van while we ate lunch at a picnic table nearby. I went to check on him shortly thereafter, and the sound of the van door opening woke him up. We joined the others at the picnic table, but Nick wasn't ready to eat yet. The diaper bag was always packed full of snacks for just such an occasion, so we went ahead and packed up our picnic.

Back in the van and off to the antique stores we went. By the time we were halfway through the best one, Nick had become decidedly cranky, due in part to his lack of lunch and an insufficient nap. Mom offered to take him out to the van where they could play and he could have a snack. After looking around a bit more, Doug and I took the girls and went out to the van to relieve Mom who went back into the antique store to find Dad. The kids had reached their tolerance level for shopping by now, and when Mom and Dad returned to the van and the kids were climbing around on its roof, we decided to call it quits and head for home.

It was about 7:00 PM when we pulled into the driveway. It was a beautiful night, cool, but we really didn't need jackets quite yet. We were all hungry, so Mom called Pizza Hut and ordered pizza for us. When Mom got in the car to go pick up the pizza, I offered to ride along with her. Doug and Dad stayed home with the kids who were happy to be able to run free after a day trapped in stores full of "pretties" that they weren't allowed to touch.

Twenty minutes later Mom and I returned home, with a large pepperoni and a medium sausage pizza warm on my lap.

The events that follow are hard to recall because I have worked so hard not to think about them. Mom had backed into the driveway and before she put the car into the garage, I was going to get out with the pizzas. I was just opening the car door when my dad came rushing towards us with a look on his face that I hope never to see on another individual, ever.

"Nick fell in the pond!" He kept going past us and went into the garage. My mind heard the words and my body responded by carrying me around to the back of the house. Somewhere along the line, something had happened to the pizzas because they were no longer in my hands. What was in my hands now was my face as I joined Doug in an agonizing scream for our son.

The image that greeted me was one that will forever replay in the minds of all of us who were there that night. Nick lay lifeless on the sidewalk just feet from the ornamental garden pond that he had fallen into. His red Looney Toons t-shirt accentuated the paleness of his features, and his eyes stared vacantly into the evening sky.

Doug was still performing CPR on Nick when the first of the rescue workers arrived a few minutes later. I think it was a fireman, and he took over CPR on Nick until the ambulance got to the house with their equipment. Mom had mercifully taken the girls into the house, and I could see them looking out the patio door crying. I can only imagine what was going through their minds at that time.

I remember standing on the sidewalk a few feet from where Nick lay. Mom and I held one another and prayed over and over for Nick to be okay, and I knew that he would be. We loved him far too much for anything bad to happen to him. This was a scare, no doubt about it, but I knew that he was going to be all right. The rescue workers were all on their hands and knees around Nick and I couldn't see what they were doing, but I think that was probably just as well. After what seemed an eternity, the paramedics were able to detect a very faint heartbeat and Nick was moved to the ambulance.

Mom stayed at the house with Allie and Kate while Dad, Doug and I followed the ambulance to Clinton's Mercy Hospital emergency room. There the staff on duty did everything in their power to bring Nick back to us. We were asked to stay in the waiting room, and periodically a nurse would come and fill us in on Nick's vitals and what was being done to help him.

While we waited, several of Mom and Dad's friends arrived. They had been at a concert in town, and one of them, a former police officer had found out by scanner about the ambulance call to Mom and Dad's house. I don't recall the exact details, but I do know that they left the concert so they could be with us in that waiting room. One of our friends, Diana, went back to the house to stay with the girls so that Mom could come be with us at the hospital. Just as Mom was arriving, the pastor from our family church got there also. Apparently someone had called him at some point in time. The waiting room was full, filled with family, friends, and prayers.

We were allowed in to see Nick once they had him stabilized. The nurse warned us ahead of time about all the tubes that he would have. My initial reaction to seeing Nick was relief, because he had his normal coloring back. Besides the tubes, one could almost imagine that he was just sleeping. The warming blankets had brought his temperature back up, and the ventilator kept him breathing well. We were allowed to stay with Nick, talking to him and touching him until the Pediatric Life Flight arrived from Iowa City. At that point we were asked to step out of the room until the Life Flight pediatrician could complete his assessments.

After what seemed an eternity, the doctor came and told us that Nick had been put on anti-seizure medication and that he hopefully wouldn't have any seizures while being transported to Iowa City. We were also given other information but, quite honestly, the whole thing is a blur to me now.

We watched as Nick was secured on the helicopter gurney. It had a special seatbelt for infants. I recall the Life Flight pediatrician talking on the phone back and forth with Iowa City a lot. The weather had taken a turn for the worse and due to lightning and thunderstorms near Iowa City, the doctors decided it would be safer to take Nick there by ambulance. We kissed Nick one last time, telling him that we loved him and that he'd be back home swinging in his swing in no time. Then he was wheeled out of the room and into the waiting ambulance.

Before Nick's doctor left to follow him into the ambulance, he gave us directions to the hospital and the location of the Pediatric Intensive Care Unit (PICU) once we got there. He told us to find someone to drive us the hour and a half to Iowa City and that there was no sense in hurrying. It would take time for the PICU staff to get Nick into his room, evaluated, and hooked up to the new equipment: a total of three hours from his time of arrival if I remember correctly.

Leaving Nick and going back to the house without him was extremely difficult. I recall getting back to the house. It was late in the night now, and the outside garden lights were on. We could hear the gurgling of the water as it circulated back into the pond from an old water pump. Such a beautiful and serene sight, and yet the location of a horrifying nightmare. The sidewalk, softly lit now by the lights surrounding the flower garden, was still damp in one place. I looked momentarily for Nick's clothes; the red shirt with the Bugs Bunny on it, his blue jeans and his little Nike shoes. Mom saw me looking and said that she had already taken them inside.

Doug and I went in the back patio door. The first thing that caught my eye was Nick's diaper bag sitting there on the desk, right where I had put it when we had gotten home from the antique stores.

The feeling that I had at that point was familiar. I had felt it one other time when Doug's dad had passed away from cancer. Nick was four months old at the time. Jay had been taken to a hospice four days after he had been hospitalized. It was late in the night and I had all of the kids back at Jay and Marlene's house in Northwood, so that Doug, his mom, and his two sisters could stay with their dad at Hospice. The kids were all sleeping, so I was by myself when I got the call that Jay had passed away. I sat there at the dining room table, looking at his shoes lying on the floor and the stuff from his pockets lying on a side table. Everything indicated that Jay had just stepped out and would be back any moment to pick up where he had left off. My mind warred within itself, because all of my memories in that house included Jay. Imagining being without him was incomprehensible.

Now, looking at the diaper bag, I again had the feeling that this horrible thing could not have really happened, not to someone I loved so deeply. Whether this was a protective mechanism in my brain, I don't know, but there was a definite dream quality to what I was feeling.

I opened the diaper bag. I wanted to be sure that everything was in it that we would need when we brought Nick home. The first thing I saw when I unzipped the bag was Nick's burpie. It was as if that little piece of cloth was the key to opening my reality. I don't know if I had cried earlier that night, but I do remember crying then. His burpie was still wet where he had been sucking on it earlier, just a few hours previously when our lives were still ideal. I put his burpie over my face and breathed deeply. I smelled my baby on that cloth and my heart ached to erase the events of the past few hours.

I honestly don't remember if the girls were even awake when we got home. I'm sure Doug and I must have talked with them. I can't imagine that we wouldn't have. I do remember packing some clothes and toiletry items to take to the hospital with us.

Once again Mom and Dad's friends helped us out. Doug N., whom I used to make chocolate malts for when I worked at an ice cream shop during high school, drove us in our van to the hospital. I remember sitting in the back, slumped down so that my head could rest on the back of the seat. I was very tired and I think I even slept part of the way. Once we got to Iowa City, another good friend of the family, Uwe, who had driven ahead of us, drove Doug N. back home in his car. This allowed us to have our van whenever we needed it.

We followed the map we were given, and made our way to the Pediatric Intensive Care Unit (PICU). We were instructed to wait in the waiting room until Nick was situated in his room.

I remember another family sitting in the waiting room. From what I could make out, their daughter had accidentally hung herself in her closet with a jump rope. The whole thing was horribly surreal. I had the definite feeling that none of the events of the past few hours were real. At any moment a nurse would walk in carrying Nick and she would say "Sorry for the inconvenience. Your little boy is just fine. I can't imagine why he was brought here in the first place."

But then when the nurse did come for us, Nick was not in her arms. He was lying in a hospital bed with tubes and wires covering him. He was wearing only a diaper, and he was so still. I could almost fool myself into thinking that wasn't really Nick lying there because Nick would not just be lying there. Even when asleep, he moved and made noises and sucked on his burpie.

We talked to Nick and touched him. I kissed him between the eyes, just above the nose. This was my favorite spot to kiss on him. Doug was able to cry, but I don't think that I did. To cry for me meant that something was wrong, and I refused to accept that Nick could be anything but fine.

We had been in the room with Nick for maybe an hour

or so when the head pediatric doctor came in. I felt very wary of him from the beginning. I sensed that he was going to tell me things that I didn't want to hear, and I was already hardening myself to what he would say.

We were taken to an examination room where a curtain was drawn so that we could have privacy. I'm sure that the doctor had done this many times, and he said things as they were, factually and clinically. He told us that Nicholas had most likely been without oxygen for about 20 minutes and that his brain would be severely damaged. He told us that 95% of these cases did not survive and that the 5% who did live would suffer from severe cerebral palsy. His words came out slowly and deliberately. He chose them carefully, but he chose them without hope and for that I hated him. To the doctor Nicholas was already a statistic, and I vowed then and there that Nick was going to prove him wrong. Nick would make a miraculous recovery. After all, we loved him too much for events to turn out differently. And so the rest of our time in the hospital I prayed and talked to Nick, hearing what I was being told, but convinced that Nick was going to beat all the odds, and I waited for that to happen.

Where Nick's doctor lacked in hope and compassion, his nurses abounded in it. They took care of him so lovingly. A stranger might have thought he was their own child. They touched him and talked to him despite the deep coma he was in. They handled him gently and took special care to see that he was as comfortable as possible. Nick's little arms were propped up on the stuffed animals that surrounded his bed and hand made quilts covered his body.

By Sunday or Monday, again I lost track of the days, Nick was moving his arms and occasionally was opening his eyes. Doug and I were convinced it was in response to our voices and our touch. Any movement on Nick's part was cause for celebration for us because we knew that his brain was beginning to work again.

We had been told that lack of oxygen causes the brain to swell and it is ultimately the pressure and swelling in the brain that causes the damage. The swelling can increase for up to five days and it isn't until the swelling has stopped that the severity of the injury can be determined. But Nick had gone from no movement to moving his arms and opening his eyes. In our book, that was progress and it was huge.

We brought Nick's burpie in from his diaper bag out in the van. He had a tube down his throat, but I knew that he would know it was there. I put a little corner of it up against his mouth and shortly thereafter he started making sucking motions. To Doug and I this was confirmation that Nick had brain function and that he had enough consciousness to know that he had his beloved burpie again.

When the doctor came in, we filled him in, quite excitedly, on what Nick had been doing. But, again, our hope was lost on him. We were informed that Nick's movements were most likely involuntary and were not a result of efforts on Nick's part. Even Nick's sucking, which was so vigorous at times that bubbles of saliva were running down his chin, the doctor said was just reflex.

That was when I decided that I would not take to heart anything that the doctor said. I do understand that doctors working with critically ill patients must keep a certain amount of detachment for their own wellbeing. After all, cases such as Nick's happen often enough that a certain amount of routineness and detachment would be expected. But for a family going through the experience for the first horrifying time, hope and encouragement are essential. Our family would have to have enough faith and hope to make up for the lack of faith and hope in a physician who maybe knew too much.

By this time Marlene had arrived for the duration and my mom and dad had come to visit with the girls. The girls were doing as well as could be expected, although I don't think they could comprehend the seriousness of what was happening with their brother. We tried to be as honest with them as we could, telling them that Nick's brain had been hurt very badly when he fell in the pond and couldn't breathe. They wanted to know why he didn't open his eyes and asked when he would come home. I wished I would have had a good answer for them because I certainly didn't like the one that I did have for them. He didn't open his eyes because his brain wasn't working correctly and we didn't know when or if Nick would be coming home.

Before Mom and Dad took the girls back home, Mom handed me an envelope. Inside were two little white rocks that Mom had found in Nick's jeans pockets. He must have picked them up and put them in there shortly before his accident. Doug and I each took one and put it in our own pockets.

Mom also told us about a tiny, perfect pink rose that had bloomed next to the pond the morning after Nick's accident. It was the only rose on a small little rose bush that they thought was dormant for the year. Its location was most likely right on the path that Nick would have taken when he went to look in the pond that day.

We had call upon call from friends and family telling us of prayer chains and vigils for Nick all over the country. We would have our miracle and Nick would come home with us to be pampered and catered to for the rest of our lives. Doug and I had already decided that he would be allowed candy for breakfast and that he could sleep in bed between us. He'd most likely be spoiled absolutely rotten, but he'd be home. He'd be smiling and laughing, and we'd be telling him how very much he was loved over and over.

We stayed in the room with Nick for the following four days, leaving only to shower, make a phone call, or occasionally to have a meal in the cafeteria. When we did leave the room, we would take a pager with us. The nurses could reach us should the need arise. I remember the unease I felt every time I left Nick's room. I almost felt like I was abandoning him. I felt guilty for a while eating because Nick could not eat. I even gave up sweets, telling Nick that we'd have our next candy bar or dessert together.

I cannot say enough about the tremendous care that we all received from the PICU nurses. These individuals came to work each day to do a job, but they did so much more than that. They were involved in an intimate way with our family and they gave us every opportunity to bond with Nick. We were able to hold him, which meant that a special chair had to be moved in to accommodate an adult, Nick, and all his trappings. At one point, a special bed was even brought in so I could lay in bed with

Nick and hold him. We were invited to be as involved with Nick's care as we wanted to be; changing his diaper or bathing him, and we were given privacy as much as possible.

There was a male nurse, Bob, who we chose to be our authority figure. He was honest as to the severity of Nick's injuries, but he was also one who said there was always hope until given proof otherwise. We could ask him questions and his responses would be honest and yet positive, so that we were always able to keep our spirits up around him. Bob would give Nick a massage with baby lotion and do range of motion exercises with him every day. His sense of humor was welcome, and he was able to produce a smile from us now and then.

We got so that we were familiar with all of Nick's monitors, and when one would beep we knew what needed to be done to stop it. The nurses and specialists continued to come and go, performing their various tests and procedures.

By Wednesday, four days after his accident, signs indicated that Nick's brain was ceasing to function. The small encouraging signs that we had been seeing off and on stopped. He didn't move his foot anymore when his toe was pinched and he didn't gag when the tube went into his lungs to clean them. He didn't open his eyes, move his arms or suck on his burpie anymore. There were also changes in his heartbeat and respiration. He was starting to rely more heavily on the help of his ventilator. These were all signs that Nick was approaching brain death and he was scheduled for a CAT scan the following morning to confirm these suspicions.

Although we knew that things were not looking good, we all continued to pray and hope for a miracle. That night I wrote in Nick's baby book on the page entitled, "A note from Mommy to Baby." I had packed all three of the kids' baby books as well as the train engine that Grandpa Jay had made for Nick. We were having electrical problems at home when we left, and in the event of a fire, I wasn't going to lose those precious things. So I wrote to Nick and told him how much we loved him and how very special he was to us.

After a sleepless night, the time came Thursday morning for Nick's CAT scan. His CAT scan was then followed by an EKG designed to assess his heart for damage. The technician let us stay in the room with him while she glued all of the electrodes to his head. It was difficult to watch dots of glue being put in his fine, blond hair. It would be hard and probably painful to get it all out. When the time came for the actual EKG, Nick was taken to a different room and we were left with an hour of wait time.

I don't remember where we waited or where we were when we were told that the results of the CAT scan were back. I do remember being led through the nurses' lounge to a conference room in the opposite hallway. There were soda cans and coffee mugs and photos of smiling children hanging on a bulletin board. All signs of happy and normal lives.

Once in the room, we sat at a long table. Bob was on my left and Doug was on my right. I had a horrible case of butterflies in my stomach and was already beginning to steel myself to anything negative they may say. Nick's doctor and two other specialists sat at the opposite end of the table and began telling us the results of Nick's tests. Their words were subdued and deliberate and I don't recall there being much eye contact with us. I think it was hard for them to tell loving and desperate parents that their baby was not going to be okay, and that their baby, would in fact, never be going home with them.

There were two CAT scan images hanging on a chart for us to see. One was of Nick's brain when he had arrived at the hospital and the other was the one taken that morning. The two images did look significantly different, even to our untrained eyes, but it wasn't until I looked at Bob and saw the tears in his eyes that I knew our prayers couldn't be answered. The doctors exchanged slight nods with one another and informed us that Nick's brain had ceased to function. I asked Bob, "Do you agree?" If there was even the tiniest amount of hope left, we could count on Bob to find it. But he shook his had and pointed at the CAT scan images and said, "There's no mistaking that proof, even for me."

There were a lot of tears after that meeting and a lot of desperation. We couldn't understand how a little boy who was loved so completely could die while some other children would grow up being abused and eventually would become abusive themselves. And Nick, who was so loving and caring and who said his prayers every night with pride, would never have a chance to pass his goodness on to others. At least that's what we thought until we were approached about donating Nick's organs.

I think it was the social worker, Sue, who first brought up the issue of organ donation. This was never a subject we had even remotely considered in relation to our children, but now it was being given to us as an option.

Throughout the nightmare of the past four days, we had been praying for God to give us the strength to deal with all that was happening. I know that we were indeed given tremendous strength, because at the point of needing to make this monumental decision, the answer for us was perfectly clear. By donating Nick's organs, organs that he no longer could use, Nick would actually be saving lives. He may even be able to save the life of another child and save other parents from having to go through the agony that we were suffering now.

Through the miracle of God, in our minds, we were able to separate Nick from his physical body, something that I was unable to do in the past when Jay had passed away. I recall picturing him, cold and alone, buried in the cemetery. I was haunted by the image of his body being in darkness and going through the process of decomposition. With Nick, however, I never imagined him still connected to his physical body that could no longer support him. The only reason I have for my change of perspective is that God helped me to see things the way that I could deal with them best. I knew that the part that I really loved about Nick, his spirit, was safe and happy and at peace in God's loving arms.

I like to think that from the moment Nick fell in the pond, God reached down and grabbed him. Nick's body may have struggled, but Nick was already safe and snug in the arms of God and our loved ones who had already crossed over. To my way of thinking, Nick's resuscitation was to give us a few more days with our son, but ultimately to provide Nick and our family with the opportunity to give the gift of life and hope to other suffering families. Our son was a gift in life and would be a hero in death.

On September 27, our decision was made and the consent forms for organ donation were filled out. Nicholas was officially declared brain dead. Both of our parents, Allie and Kate, and Doug's sisters were at the hospital to tell Nick good-bye. I don't think the girls realized the permanence of their good-byes with their brother. We had tried our best to explain to them that Nick would not be coming home with us, that his injuries could not get better. Allie did cry just for a moment as she said, "I'm not going to have a brother anymore?" Neither of the girls knew how to deal with what they were feeling and after they had kissed him and patted him one last time, they went to the waiting room with their grandparents to play with the toys.

I think the hardest thing Doug and I have ever done was to walk out that door and leave our baby behind. We kissed him a million times, shocked at how cold his little forehead had become. I held his hand. It lay limp and lifeless, and yet still warm, in my hand. I thought how very wrong all of this must be.

I couldn't take my eyes off of Nicholas as we walked out the hospital room door. He lay there so quietly and still and yet his chest was rising and falling with each breath he was given, and I could still feel the warmth of him on my skin. "See you later, Buddy." Doug and I held hands and sobbed together as we walked down the hallway. The nurses on duty who had worked with Nick and who had gotten to know us so very well, all came out and gave us hugs good-bye. They had tears in their eyes, too, and I thought again how very special these people were. To see a child get well and go home was one thing, but to watch a family going home for the last time without their child was quite another. These professionals dealt with loss regularly and yet they had never become hardened to it. We felt their genuine grief and disappointment that events hadn't turned out differently.

The ride back to Mom and Dad's house was a very quiet one. The girls sat in the back, secure in their car seats, eating candy that Grandma had given them. Doug and I both were very aware of the empty car seat directly behind us and of the diaper bag that was sitting on the floor in front of it. The contents were still untouched except for Nick's burpie which he still had tucked under his arm. The outfit I had packed to bring Nick home in was also still at the hospital. The nurses had promised to dress him for me after his surgery; his favorite clothes, jeans, long sleeved t-shirt with the puppy on it and white athletic socks. His shoes, I imagine were still drying somewhere at Mom and Dad's house.

When we returned to my parents' house in Clinton, we entered through the side garage door, on purpose avoiding the beautiful, but fateful flower garden and pond out back. Food, brought by friends of the family, covered the counter, and Nick's get well flowers and balloons sat on the kitchen table. There was a sweet irony about the "get well" messages. I don't think that anyone had considered the possibility that Nick would not be okay.

I took the bag with all of our things from the hospital to where we stayed downstairs. Nick's stuffed animals were on top, and on impulse, I picked one up and smelled it. I inhaled my baby's smell. It was the smell of the lotion that Bob had used when massaging Nick's motionless limbs. It was the smell that had become Nick's own over the past four days.

Out of sheer exhaustion we did sleep that night, but waking up to our reality was a nightmare. We packed our things and were ready to leave for home when we got a phone call. It was Sue, the social worker from the hospital. She was calling to tell us that Nick's surgery had gone well. At 2:00 AM that morning they had "harvested" Nick's liver, intestine, heart, and kidneys. The Organ Donor Network had been unable to find a recipient for his lungs, but the other organs were already being transplanted. The news was bittersweet. It conjured up images of Nicholas lying in surgery with his chest spread open. But even as his organs could no longer serve his body, we knew that they would be saving the lives of others. Maybe the lives of children whose parents were praying not to experience what we were going through. That thought was a powerfully positive one, and it was the thought that I would find myself clinging to time and again.

Our call concluded and anxious to get home, mostly to "get it over with," the four of us got in the van and drove a very quiet, very numb, three hours home. Mom and Dad were going to follow about an hour behind us, so that we would have time to ourselves once we got home. In my mind I could already picture Nick's little, black play shoes and his boots in the mud room. Those would be the first of many reminders to greet us.

As we drove up our drive, however, it became apparent how many memories with Nick occurred outside of our home. There was the swing and the sand box and the pile of dirt that he liked to dig in so much. They all looked very still and empty, and I dreaded what awaited us once we got inside. I craved everything of

Nick's and yet it was tremendously painful to revisit so many recent memories, to realize that was all they were, memories. We would never see him in the swing or the sandbox again, and he would never again be crouched down with the little shovel and bucket digging in the dirt. Once more it occurred to me that this all had to be a horrible, horrible dream that I would wake up from soon.

Doug and I entered the house arm in arm. We passed Nick's shoes just where he had taken them off. I noticed the chunks of dirt still attached to their bottoms, the reason that they had been left home in the first place. In the kitchen sink was the sippy cup that he had been drinking out of before we had left for Clinton. I recall being irritated that I had to leave a dirty cup in the sink.

Entering the family room we could see Nick's bucket of toys, his cars and balls and favorite books. We kept going, wanting to get the tour over with, and so came to Nick's bedroom. His bed was still turned down, and his pajamas were lying near his pillow. On the Winnie the Pooh pillowcase, I could faintly make out the marks where he had drooled in his sleep.

Doug and I sat on the bed and looked around us. Everything was where it should be. The big red barn was on the floor in the corner with the giant Elmo sitting on top of it. Next to that was the stuffed dinosaur that Nick had gotten for his second birthday three months ago. On his dresser was the Winnie the Pooh nightlight and the ceramic Pooh figurine. His wipes, also in a Pooh container, sat in the center with the diaper ointment and hand soap nearby. Under one window sat the beanie baby shelf that Grandpa Jay had been making shortly before he passed away. The little blond- haired boy beanie that we had gotten at Adventure Land, who wore a t-shirt saying "I Love Nick," sat on the top shelf. Under the other window was the wooden potty seat that Nick liked to sit on, but had never used. Nick's rocking motorcycle, also made by Grandpa Jay, sat motionless in front of the open closet door. The door always remained open because Nick's toys were on a shelf inside. There was his fire engine and the Sesame Street saxophone. His board books were in a laundry basket sitting on top of his toy box, and hanging above on the bar, were Nick's clothes. It dawned on me that the next outfit that I picked out for him would be for his funeral service.

Doug and I both were completely overwhelmed. Doug cried and I wanted to, but couldn't. I shook my head back and forth in continued denial of the events that had taken place. I think I halfway was expecting the hospital to call and tell us that somehow Nick had made a miraculous recovery, one they just couldn't explain, but we could come pick him up immediately. I even went so far as to imagine my tears of joy when I saw him next and he smiled at me and said "Hi, Mommy." I would run to him and pick him up then fall to my knees with tears streaming down my face. I would kiss Nick and thank God for giving our son back to us. But that phone call never came.

I remember standing by the kitchen sink when Mom and Dad arrived. I was doing something, I'm not sure what, but all of a sudden I could smell Nick very clearly. I told Mom as much as she came in the door. It was the smell of the baby lotion again. I was very excited at the thought that this was Nick's way of telling me that he was still with me, but I also wanted to be sure that there wasn't another explanation. I went through a checklist of sorts in my head; I had showered since being at the hospital and had changed my clothes. I could think of no other explanation for what I smelled except that Nick wanted me to know he was there. I whispered to him, "I can smell you, Buddy." Although a skeptic might say the smell was all in my head, quite frankly, I would never want someone to talk me out of something that I believe to be true and found tremendously comforting. I thanked Nick and hoped that would be the first of many signs from Nick letting me know that he was okay.

While all of this was taking place, Doug had been on the phone with Pastor Lynn, setting the date for the funeral. After hanging up, Doug informed us that there was already a funeral scheduled at our church for Monday, Oct. 1, so we would have to have Nick's service on Tuesday or Wednesday. It was already Friday, and I understood that arrangements and notifying people would take some time, but there was no way that I was going to leave my baby sitting in a storage area until Tuesday or Wednesday. I had Doug call Pastor Lynn back and told him that we didn't care what time of the day Nick's service was, but it had to be on Monday. Pastor Lynn called the funeral director and explained our feelings, and although it would be a lot of work for him, he agreed to let us have the service on Monday morning at 10:00 AM.

Mom helped me clean a little bit for the people who were expected to come by the house. And come they did. Friends stopped by with meals, paper products, baked goods, and entire bags of groceries. (This in addition to the friends who had come while we were still in Iowa

City. They had mowed the grass, fixed our electrical problem, bought us a new bag of rabbit food, and even cleaned out the cat litter box for us.) Our propane supplier came by the house to fill our tank for us, and as he was leaving said there would be no charge. He told us that we didn't realize how many friends we had, but I think we were beginning to.

Doug and I were eternally grateful for the outpourings of support we received, but we found it virtually impossible to face these people as they came to the house. At one point Doug and I were sitting out in the backyard on the wooden swing. It faced the kids' swing set, and I think we both were visualizing the last time our children had all been playing on it together. We heard a car coming up our gravel drive, and in the next instant we were both running for the house. I know the driver had seen us, but we just couldn't talk with anyone. We couldn't look in the eyes of our friends and see their pain and sympathy, and we couldn't yet talk about what had happened and answer the questions that surely would arise. Marlene arrived later in the day, so while Doug and I hid in the interior of the house, our parents greeted people, took in the generous offerings that they had brought and recorded the items in a book for us so that we could write thank- you notes later on.

That night we got a phone call. There were so many calls that our parents had been answering them for us. This call, however, was one that we took. It was Amy, one of the very special nurses from the hospital in Iowa City. She called to tell Doug and me about how Nick's surgery had gone. She told us that once we had left, she had gone in and sat with Nick whenever she had the opportunity.

She said she talked to him and kissed him because that is what she would have done if he were her child. Nick's organ retrieval surgery had been at 2:00 AM Friday morning. His organs had all been remarkably healthy and doctors were able harvest all of the organs for recipients who were waiting. Amy continued to tell us that after the surgery was completed, she and another nurse had continued to talk to Nick as they dressed him in the clothes that I had left. Then Amy had carried Nick out of the room, saying that she didn't want to see him leave on a gurney. Words will never describe the gratitude that we feel for this very special individual. We will be grateful to her for her love and compassion always.

Chapter 3

Saturday morning rolled around and with it the daunting task of making more arrangements. My dad went with Doug and me to the funeral home to talk with the funeral director about details pertaining to the funeral. The funeral parlor was beautifully decorated and under different circumstances, I would have been duly impressed. Fred sat us down in seats surrounding his desk and began to tell us what we needed to know.

He had already picked Nicholas up from Iowa City where his body had been prepared by another mortician. Fred explained that great care had been taken with Nick's appearance and that, except for the sore spot on one of Nick's cheeks from the tape that had been holding the vent tube, Nick would look very much like he was supposed to, precious. They were unable to cross Nick's arms over his chest. I don't recall what the reason was anymore, but his arms would be at his sides.

Then Fred handed me a sack containing the clothes that Nick had been dressed in at the hospital. I looked inside the bag and was horrified to see Nick's precious burpie in there. Somewhere, someone had not been informed that Nick was to have that with him at all times. I explained to Fred about Nick's burpie and he promised to tuck the precious belonging back under Nick's arm. All of Nick's other belongings were folded neatly inside the bag and I was somewhat disappointed to see that his clothes had been laundered. They may have still smelled like him. Then Fred asked me how I combed Nick's hair and asked for the clothes that I had brought to dress him in.

I had chosen Nick's tan pants which he wore to church and a long sleeved, collared shirt with pictures of tools all over it. Fred was glad to see our choice of shirt. It would tuck up under Nick's chin to cover the incision left from the organ retrieval surgery. I had picked out tan socks and the little brown boat shoes to match Nick's pants, but the more I thought about it, I realized that no one would see those anyway, so I chose his favorite white athletic socks and the Nikes that he had been wearing when he fell in the pond. They would be much more comfortable. Nick, I thought, probably would have picked his black play shoes, but I just couldn't part with them.

Next Fred took us to the adjoining room and showed us the little white casket that would be Nick's resting place. We all had great difficulty looking at that tiny white box. I think Doug and my dad cried, but once again, all I could do was shake my head. This just couldn't be happening.

We sat back down in our seats by Fred's desk, and in a daze, completed our business with him. We named our casket bearers; my brother, Eric; Doug's brother-in-law, Doug L.; and our good friends, Wayne and Renald. Then we told him the songs that we had picked out the night before; "Jesus Loves Me," "Hymn of Promise," and "Come Follow Me." We had decided that we wanted Nick's service to be uplifting, a celebration of his life. There was already enough sadness surrounding his loss without a grim and depressing service.

I actually didn't want Nick's service to resemble a funeral at all. I felt a little angry and frustrated with the idea of having to have a funeral to begin with. I didn't ask for this to happen to our son, and now I was being forced to go through this thing that I didn't want to go through and it was out of my hands to change it. So all I could do was ask that the service be as uplifting and non-funeral like as possible. Pastor Lynn was very supportive of my feelings, and I was pleased with the ideas that he shared with Doug and me.

Fred explained to us every detail of the funeral proceedings. He was very professional and yet at the same time he, like us, was having a hard time dealing with the nature of this particular service. He himself had lost an eight-month old daughter, so was familiar with the pain that we were feeling. Our business concluded, the time came for payment, but instead of the traditional list of expenses, all we were given was the bill for the tiny white casket. Everything else was being donated. I was able to cry then in humble thanks for the tremendous kindness and generosity we were being shown.

After the funeral home, we went home, picked up our moms and the girls and headed to Marshalltown to pick out flowers. The drive over was beautiful. It was early fall and the leaves were beginning to change. The weather was unseasonably warm and the sky was clear and blue. I loved days like this and if I allowed my mind to drift, I could almost imagine that all was right with the world.

The florist shop was full of beautiful arrangements and as I looked around I wished that we could be here to pick out anything except flowers for our son's funeral. We were taken to a little sitting area near the back of the store and were given books to look at containing various casket sprays. The store attendant asked if the girls would like to pick out some flowers for Nick themselves. They thought that was a wonderful idea and so she took them, hand in hand, to the cut flower area.

Looking through three large binders of floral arrangements was a daunting task. Was one obliged to look through them, page by page, to find the perfect one? Dad was my savior at this point, because I think he was thinking along the same lines as I was. "This is really uncomfortable, let's just pick something and go." After all, aren't all flowers beautiful?

The girls came back then with the florist and were beaming with pride at the cut flowers they had chosen for their brother. Rather than look through all the books, I told her what I was thinking of and she opened one of the books to the very page we needed, a small spray of tiny, blue and white roses, greenery and baby's breath. That would be just right.

Mom, Dad and Marlene picked out a heart shaped form that would be covered with red and white roses. It would have a "Grandson" ribbon on it. Other flowers were picked out to be from Nick's six living great-grandparents, and I chose a silk flower arrangement to be from Eric and Vickie. I wanted at least one arrangement that I could not kill and would be able to keep forever.

We went back home, ate lunch, and then Doug, Dad and I went to meet the man at the cemetery to pick out a gravesite. Doug and I already had decided to purchase three plots at once. We both wanted to be buried next to Nick. He would be in the middle, so that we would be in the same order that we were when we used to all be in bed together. The plots we chose were towards the back of the cemetery. They would be far from the road and somewhat secluded. The view was pretty; the nearby fence separated the cemetery grounds from a pasture and woodlands that we knew surrounded a small lake and county park. It would be a nice and tranquil spot to visit.

Nick's visitation was scheduled for Sunday evening, so by Sunday afternoon we had a house full of family who had come to be with us. Inside, there was standing room only and several conversations could be heard going on simultaneously in the kitchen and family room. The kids were all enjoying being together, so the sounds of laughter and playing could be heard mingled with the sounds of crying and talking.

I felt somewhat removed from what was going on around me and wasn't quite sure what to do with myself. I didn't want to join in with those conversing about the tragedy of what had happened with Nick and I didn't want to be around those who were laughing with the kids. So, for awhile, I went in our bedroom, closed the door, and crawled under the covers of our bed. Maybe helplessness was partly what I was feeling. But I think I also felt angry and desperate. Life was continuing on at a frantic pace and all I wanted was some time to breathe and to think of how our family would go on with life without our precious little Nick.

As I lay there, praying for the strength to get through the next two days, I started thinking of how this was going to affect, not only me and my family, but our extended family and our friends as well. I knew that Nick's death had shaken the faith of a lot of them, and they were questioning why God would let this happen to Nick and our family. I wanted these loved ones to know that God had not made this horrible thing happen. No one was being punished and God was crying with us for our loss. Why Nick couldn't have had the miraculous recovery we prayed so hard for, we will never know. I liked to think that Nick was maybe an old soul who had learned and accomplished all he needed to do here. He had achieved his goal and had earned his right to go to heaven.

This was the kind of thinking that was allowing me to be "okay," and I wanted to share it with my family. So I decided that I would write my feelings down and give Pastor Lynn the written copy to read at Nick's service the next morning. I remember feeling somewhat revived with a sense of purpose after that and I got up out of bed. I saw one of Nick's baby pictures, a close-up of his face; a big toothless smile and drool running down his chin, on my dresser mirror as I was reaching for the door. It reminded me that I wanted to take a couple of pictures with us to the visitation that night. There would be some people there who had never met Nick, and I wanted them to see him smiling and full of life.

I also chose items that had been special to Nick that would stay in his arms for eternity: a small, soft football from Mom and Dad's house, a cross-stitch that Allie had made for Nick that had his name and birth date on it,

Nick's favorite book, *Cars, Cars, Cars,* a family picture which I had written on the back of, "We love you, Buddy! Mommy, Daddy, Allie and Kate," a second picture of Nick with his sisters, all wearing bunny faces, and of course, his Burpie.

Nick's visitation that night was a surreal event. The church was filled with beautiful flowers, and pictures of Nick surrounded the tiny white casket. Seeing his precious little body for the first time...I can't even describe what I felt. I think a part of me chose to view him as though he were just sleeping. I couldn't keep my hands off of him; I kept smoothing the silky blond hair on his forehead. I remember thinking that I had never seen it quite so neat and perfect before. I had the urge to mess it up so it would look as if he had been tossing in bed all night on his Winnie the Pooh pillow.

His shirt was neatly tucked in and again, that just struck me as not quite right, because his shirts never stayed tucked in for long. His arms were to his sides and his little hands were so still. I tucked his burpie under his right arm, as close to its rightful place as I could get it.

I kissed Nick repeatedly in my favorite spot right between his eyes. He smelled of powder and was so cold, but otherwise if I kept my eyes closed, he felt just the way he should.

People began to arrive and the next two hours was a procession of hugs, kisses and condolences. People didn't know what to say to us and that was just as well because we wouldn't have known how to respond to them anyway. I clutched one of Nick's burpies in my hand the entire evening, using it as a source of strength perhaps. Whenever there was a lull in the line, Doug and

I would go back to our son's side, leaning on one another for support. I tried to memorize every last detail on Nick's body, knowing that after 10:00 AM the following day I would never be able to see him physically again.

I remember seeing a tiny black speck of dirt, or possibly pond debris, in his ear that I had seen in the same spot at the hospital. For some odd reason, I found that comforting. Maybe he had gotten it in his ear the last time he had been playing outside. It was a link somehow to the life of normalcy that we had so recently left behind, a transport back in time to happier days.

But then on his left cheek was the sore left behind from one of the tubes that had been part of his life support at the hospital. The mortician had done a good job of covering it with make-up, but it remained a very real reminder that all was not normal and happy. Our baby was not just sleeping; he had gone on to heaven where he had important things waiting for him. The problem was, though, we were not ready for him to move on. And so we did our best to hold ourselves together and to prepare ourselves for the next day when we would have a funeral for our two-year-old son and watch him buried in the cemetery.

The following morning, I got ready, putting on my best dress. It was the same dress that I had bought to wear to a Christmas party the year before, but had instead worn to my father-in-law's funeral. Now the second time that I was wearing it was to the funeral of my son.

Somewhere between getting dressed and arriving at the church, I'm sure I got the girls ready and probably ate some breakfast. I don't recall the drive in to town, but I do remember that it was a very pretty day. It was October first, and the trees were already splendid in the colors of fall. The temperature was perfect, the sun was shining, and the birds were singing. I was thinking how I would have given anything to turn back the clock and change the events of the past days.

The closest time I can recall to feeling anywhere near the way I was feeling, was the morning Doug was driving me in to Ames to be induced with Allison. I was absolutely terrified and had the unmistakable urge to jump out of the car at the stop sign and run. I had that same feeling of dread and desperation this morning. The difference being, in the first instance, although I was scared, I knew I would be bringing a beautiful life into this world. And this day, I was watching a beautiful life leave it. But all the same, I had the feeling of wanting to turn away and run from what I knew had to happen. Like a kid whose response to an unfavorable situation is, "This isn't fair, and you can't make me do it!" Except that I was an adult and I knew that I had to do it.

We arrived at the church at our designated time and Fred instructed us where to park so that we would be the first car to leave in the funeral procession. By the planning and organization involved, one might have been fooled into thinking there was a grand affair taking place, and we were the guests of honor, entitled to special VIP treatment. I guess by some stretch of the imagination, we were the guests of honor. The cars parked around the church were there because of us, and the people walking up the stairs to the sanctuary were again, there because of us.

But I would have given anything to not be in this position.

I almost resented the presence and support of all those people; only, here I think, because I was so helpless to stop the event that had brought them here. If, at this moment in time, there were no people walking up the steps, and no cars parked up and down the street, then Nicholas would not be lying in a coffin upstairs, and there would not be a funeral for him. Nicholas would instead be buckled in his car seat in the middle seat of the van, right where he should be. We could be on our way to a picnic or something.

As much as I tried to clear this nightmare from my reality, it would not go away, and so we made our way up the front steps and into the church, there to see our son for the very last time.

People cleared a path for us as we neared the doorway to the sanctuary. It was as if an invisible field had grown up around us and was pushing away all of those who were too close. Through the door, I could see the little coffin. The lid was open and the family pictures were again sitting out. I found it very difficult to breath and thought that this would be a really good time to wake up from this particularly bad dream.

Doug and the girls were beside me as we stepped up to the casket. What was going through my mind was, now that I'm here, how am I going to leave? How do I walk away from my baby, knowing that I'm never going to see him again in this lifetime? I'm his mother and we need one another, so how can I just walk away from him? I kissed Nick and touched him; one hand on his soft, perfectly combed hair and the other on his too firm chest. I talked to him and told him how much I loved him. I studied his little hands trying to commit to memory every detail. I wanted to be able to close my eyes and see every fingernail and every crease in those chubby hands.

I became aware of a gentle nudging at my back. I stepped aside for a moment so that Doug could lift the girls up to see their brother. The girls were unsure of what they were supposed to do. We told them to just talk to Nick and tell him anything that they wanted to tell him. We also told them that they could touch him and give him a kiss if they wanted to. Allison touched Nick's cheek and immediately pulled her hand back, a disturbed look on her face. It wasn't what she was used to feeling, not the same warm, pink cheeks that smiled and laughed with her.

It crossed my mind how Allie and Kate were too young to have to deal with such personal tragedy, and I prayed to God to give Doug and me the strength to provide them with their "good ol' days."

More and more people were arriving and the church was beginning to fill up behind us. Again people were trying to give us as much space as they could, which was difficult given the size of the entryway. It was time for us to go downstairs and wait with the other family members until it was time for us to enter the sanctuary for the ceremony.

The downstairs fellowship room was already full of our family and closest friends. The last time that we had all been together like this was for Nick's baptism. Aunts and uncles, nieces and nephews, grandparents and cousins, all of them who were healthy enough and able to make the trip were there. Some sat, some stood, many reminisced with other family whom they hadn't seen in awhile, but I think everyone was in a state of shock that they were in this room awaiting the funeral of their beloved Nicholas.

It was hard for me to keep in mind that I was not the only one who had suffered a loss. It was very easy for me to get lost in my own grief and desperation, so that I would forget that there were others around me sharing my pain. I wasn't the only one to lose a precious loved one and I admit to even feeling angry at times when I heard someone else crying for Nick. I felt like saying, "What are you crying for?! He's my baby!"

With the precision of an army sergeant, the time came when Fred called us to line up for the procession back upstairs to the sanctuary. Doug, the girls and I were first up the stairs. I recall that my heart was pounding and I again felt like I needed to turn around and run away. At the top of the stairs we rounded the corner and there again sat the little white coffin, this time back dropped by a room full of people with their heads bowed down.

Our friend Shawn was playing the piano, a Scott Joplin song called "Solace." Doug and I again went to Nick's side and I touched him one more time knowing that this would be the final time that I saw his precious little face, with the perfect little eyes and nose and ears, the little mouth and forehead that I had kissed a million times and would never kiss again. The little hands, so motionless that had held mine just a few short days ago as we had walked down to get the mail.

I stepped aside so that Allison and Kate could talk to Nick and touch him one more time. They nervously reached their little hands up and gave Nick a pat. Kate said something to Nick about "I hope you get better soon so we can play." Allie was just pulling her hand back with a surprised look on her face. "Mom, why is his face sticky?" Their innocent questions pulled me back for a moment into their reality. So young to have suffered such a loss, and they didn't even fully realize yet how real this all was.

I became aware of our family lined up behind us and knew that the time had come for us to go sit down, but I couldn't seem to walk away. How could I leave his side when I knew it was for the last time? I felt almost as if I were abandoning Nick. He was so little to be without his Mommy.

I made the attempt to walk away and I could see out of the corner of my eye, my mom and dad moving into the spot I had just left. Almost as if I had no control over my body, I turned and nearly ran over my family in a desperate attempt to get back to Nick's side. The tears that I had been unable to cry all morning suddenly made an appearance as I buried my face in Nick's hair. He smelled of powder and his forehead was unnaturally cold and firm. I put my hands on his little cheeks and looked into his closed eyes, willing him to open them and prove that this had all been a horrible mistake. I promised God that I wouldn't blame anyone for putting us all through this if Nick would just open his big blue eyes and grin at me. "Hi, Mommy."

My little girls were clutching their daddy's hands, unable to comprehend what had just happened to their lives. My husband's eyes mirrored the same pain that was in my heart. I couldn't understand why God had allowed Nick to die. I believed that God could perform miracles, so why didn't our family deserve one? The little girl in the room next to Nick's at the hospital had hung herself in her closet with a jump rope. I had hugged and cried with her mother, but in the end that little girl had gone home with her family.

As I pulled my hands off of Nick's cheeks, I had the perverse thought that hopefully I hadn't messed up his make-up. I kissed him one last time between the eyes and made sure that he was holding his burpie, then I told him, "See you later, Buddy," and I walked away to the waiting hands of my two precious daughters.

I don't really recall who was at the funeral, except for family members. Not liking to be the center of attention under the best of circumstances, I really didn't like being the center of attention now, so as we were directed to our place in the pews, I chose to watch the carpet under my feet. Then we sat together as a family, an incomplete family, and we waited for the service to begin.

Doug and I looked at the beautiful flowers sent by friends and loved ones that had been placed so carefully at the front of the church. An 8x10 of Nick, complete with scabbed knee, and the wooden train engine that Grandpa Jay had made for him were artfully arranged between the flowers. I knew that everything looked very nice and at the same time I shook my head ever so slightly. Doug and I looked at one another, and although we didn't exchange any words, both knew what the other was thinking. How could this be happening, and how will we ever be okay again?

As Shawn continued to play the organ, Pastor Lynn walked slowly down the aisle and took his place at the pulpit. He carried a children's book in his hands, a book called *The Fall of Freddy the Leaf*. In keeping with our wishes that this not be the typical, "Old Rugged Cross" funeral, he explained to all in attendance that he was going to read this book. Since there was no easy way of explaining to a sanctuary full of despondent people why God would allow Nicholas's life to be cut so short, he instead chose to remind us that death is just another stage that we all go through. Death may be scary to contemplate because we haven't experienced it firsthand, but it is really just the natural and beautiful stage following life. When it came time for Pastor Lynn to read the letter that I had written, I held my breath hoping that it would reach, not only the ears, but the hearts of those who so desperately needed to hear it:

Terrible tragedies can sometimes shake a person's faith in God. We must know that God does not make these events happen; he is crying right beside us. We can't understand why it was Nick's turn to go, and we can't understand why he wasn't granted the miraculous recovery that we had all prayed so hard for. We can know that God had a reason for taking Nick so soon, and because of our faith in God, we must accept it.

We will think of Nick often and what might have been, and we will grieve over his loss, but life will go on for all of us. We all deserve lives filled with joy and happiness, and we need to permit ourselves to seek those lives. As we do live though, we must remember to show others our love and compassion; to tell our loved ones how important they are; that they are not taken for granted.

It is a great comfort to us that Nicholas left us knowing he is dearly loved and cherished. He had a very happy and full life despite how short it was. Nick will continue to live on in our hearts and memories, but he will also live on in the bodies of three other suffering people. His kidneys were a perfect match for a 48-year-old woman. His liver and intestine were given to a 2-year-old little girl and his heart is now inside a 3-month-old baby girl. We all must pray for these individuals that they will live long and happy lives.

We thank God for all of those who gave so much of themselves in trying to bring Nick back to us, for all of those who prayed for us, cried with us and offered us overwhelming support. Your thoughts and prayers are truly felt and we are blessed by every one of you.

Nick's funeral was beautiful and horrendous. Pastor Lynn did his best to keep the service as uplifting as he could and, despite his tear-filled eyes and the momentary quavering of his voice, he did a good job. We sang the song I had picked out, "Come Follow Me," a song I had sung with the church choir. I recall that I started singing before everyone else. Under normal circumstances, I would have been completely embarrassed, but this day, although I noticed, I truly didn't care.

Once the service was mercifully over, Fred directed the four casket bearers to their places at the sides of the tiny casket. My brother, Eric, Doug's brother-in-law Doug L., and our good friends, Wayne and Renald, each held the handles, and without much effort, carried our son and his precious belongings up the aisle. As they passed, I kissed my fingers and lightly touched them to the cold, hard exterior of Nick's casket. The finality that the lid of that box would never be opened again hit me, and it occurred to me that I would never see Nick's precious face in person again until the day of my own passing and he was there to greet me. On that day I would run into his waiting arms and never look back.

But for now, there was a hole at the cemetery waiting to receive his body and we were being ushered up the aisle and to our waiting cars. Again, I chose not to look into any of the eyes that were watching us leave. The pain and sympathy in the room was thick, and although it was warm and comforting, it was also unwanted and smothering. We should never have been on the receiving end of such pity. This gathering of people should be here attending the funeral of someone who had lived a long full life. Someone deeply loved and who would be missed, but at the same time, we would be saying, "Well, he lived a long, full and happy life, and now he won't have to suffer anymore." That we could understand. But to lose a two-year-old child who was healthy, happy, and just beginning to live? Understanding that was much more difficult.

Our van was first in line behind the hearse, and although it wasn't cold outside, Fred had started the van for us so that it was nice and warm inside. We drove the four blocks to the cemetery and parked just feet away from the blue awning that loomed over a large gaping hole in the ground. There was a row of chairs, draped in blue cloth, lined up front and center. I had stood behind chairs such as these several times, always surrounded by mourners quietly blowing their noses. Being short, I would have to peer between shoulders to get a glimpse of the minister and the casket. But now I was being ushered to the blue chairs for a completely unobscurred view of the proceedings. Behind me gathered the others. I could hear the sniffing and the purses opening, then the rummaging for a Kleenex. I wanted to cry. I wanted others to see me cry, because that's what mothers do when their babies die. But I couldn't cry. The Kleenex in my one hand remained dry, while the burpie that I squeezed tightly in my other hand was damp with perspiration.

When the snake of cars coiled around the cemetery had ceased to move, Pastor Lynn took his place beside Nick's casket and started the graveside service. I don't remember a word of what he said, but I do remember that it was very "funeral-like." Sitting in a blue chair in a cemetery full of headstones and with our child's casket three feet in front of me, It was hard to imagine that I was anywhere other than at our child's funeral.

Despite the grayness of quiet emotion, the sky remained bright blue and there was a warm, gentle breeze blowing in from the south. As we got in our van, I wanted more than anything to go home where I could sit outside on the bench swing with Doug and watch our kids play on the swing set. It would be a good day to play outside. I might even let them get out the squirt bottles so they could squirt each other with water one last time before the weather turned too cold. Nick wouldn't squirt anyone with his, however. He preferred squirting the trees and flowers. And the girls usually knew better than to squirt him. If Nick did happen to get wet, either on purpose or by accident, he'd get mad. Then he'd come over to me so I could dry him off. He probably would have his feelings hurt, so he'd sit between Doug and I and we'd swing together, his squirt bottle still in his hands.

As Doug drove out of the cemetery, he turned left heading out of town. I wondered if he had read my mind and wanted to go home too. But then he turned again and I knew he was taking the back way back to the church. All of the other cars behind us turned right and headed back to the church the way they had come.

In the fellowship hall, the ladies of the church had prepared a light lunch. Family and friends filled the downstairs room, and before long there was the familiar buzz of countless conversations taking place simultaneously. People filed through the food line, filling their plates with ham sandwiches, chips and cake. Some of the tension had been lifted, I think, given that the unpleasant task of the funeral had been completed.

I feel that I am being unfair sometimes when I insinuate that the others just picked up and went on as though nothing had happened. I know that everyone in the room was dealing with their own loss of Nick. I was so immersed in my own loss, however, that watching people eat, smile and converse made me angry. I felt as though Nick's funeral had turned into a bonus family reunion. I couldn't eat or smile and I had no desire to converse, so how could anyone else? Didn't the world know that Nick was dead?! But then the world goes on, doesn't it. How to go on? That would be the problem.

I'm pretty sure that Doug, the girls and I left early. The next thing I remember is taking off the dreaded pantyhose and putting on my favorite jeans and t-shirt. I felt guilty somehow putting on my old comfortable clothes. I had second thoughts at that moment about the clothes that I had chosen for Nick to be buried in. My jeans and t-shirt were a comfort to me and I regretted that I had chosen Nick's church clothes for him. I wished I would have chosen his favorite clothes, also jeans and a t-shirt. My moment of regret passed quickly as I realized that Nick had more important things to do than to worry about the clothes that his earthly body had been buried in. Yes, Nick wouldn't care. Angels would be occupied with more meaningful thoughts and tasks.

Among those who had come to lend support to us were my "new" grandma and her family from Cleveland. They had arrived on Sunday, so were able to be at Nick's visitation and funeral. I know I mentioned Hazel and Herman earlier, but I do so again now because they are so worth mentioning. Doug and I both have been blessed with wonderful and loving families, and in 1993, Hazel and Herman and their son Don and his family were added to the list. Hazel had given my dad up for adoption just after his birth as that was the only option available to her at the time. Fifty-some years later, we have been reunited and have been making up for lost time ever since. When Hazel, Herman, Don and Linda heard of Nick's passing, they dropped what they were doing, got plane tickets, and flew from Ohio to be with us. Maybe partly because they, too, had lost a son and brother in the war in Vietnam, but mostly, I think because they have come to love us just as we have come to love them.

Anyway, wearing my comfortable clothes, I made my way through the throngs of family members who were trying to find a place to be in our cozy house. I didn't stop to visit and no one tried to talk to me. In the kitchen Mom, Marlene, Hazel and Doug's sisters were setting food out on the counter. There seemed to be an infinite supply of sandwiches, chips, bars, breads and paper supplies that friends and acquaintances had generously dropped off. I should have stayed and visited. I should have stayed and been a gracious hostess, but I didn't. I slipped outside without as much as a word to anyone. Outside I could breathe.

Doug, Dad, Eric, Herman, and Don were standing just outside in front of the garage. Dad looked at me with tears in his eyes and gave me an emotion filled hug. Don was next to give me a hug, and then hand in hand with my "new" uncle, our little group walked together over to the fire pit and sat down at the picnic tables that had been the site of so many happy family gatherings. I don't know what we talked about, but it was nice, easy conversation. Hazel soon joined us and the two of us sat side-by-side on top of the child-size picnic table hand-made, again, by Jay. I think I felt a special bond with her at that time. We were both mothers who loved and had lost a child.

Eventually, we heard the sound of cars starting and people talking. It was time for people to go home. I really did feel badly that I hadn't spent time visiting with them, but I hoped that they would understand. Facing a tragedy first-hand, one can learn a lot about oneself. Whereas some would want to be surrounded by friends and loved ones, being hugged and consoled, I just felt a need to be alone. I would have friends later who would have their feelings hurt because I didn't call on them for comfort and take them up on their offers to "get out of the house." I could understand that they themselves would have need of others put in the situation that I was in, but my needs were different and I had to hope that they could understand that. The only things that I needed at the moment were my family and a whole lot of time to develop my coping mechanisms.

By Tuesday morning our remaining family had left for home, and Allison and Kate were ready to get back to school and get back to life. They had missed two weeks of classes and were craving the normalcy of their previous lives. It was with tremendous difficulty that I watched Allison get on the bus. I felt almost a desperate need to keep her home with me so that I could protect her from all of the dangers of the world. But I stuck to my silent vow to give the girls as much of their lives back as was possible and that would include allowing them to leave the house without me.

Doug went with me to drive Kate to preschool later that morning. I walked her to the door of the church where her teacher was greeting students as they arrived. Mrs. MacIntosh had both of the girls for preschool and it dawned on me that Nick would never get to be in her class. A fortunate child encounters many great teachers throughout their school careers. Mrs. MacIntosh was one of those great teachers. Always loving and caring, she had come to Nick's visitation two short nights ago to lend support to our family, specifically to the girls. She had brought with her two glass vases of tiny pink roses and baby's breath, one for Allie and one for Kate. The girls had been delighted.

I gave Kate a kiss and tried to have a steady voice as I told her, "I love you, Honey." Then I handed Kate over into her teacher's care. Mrs. MacIntosh gave me a hug, sensing, I think, my reluctance to leave Kate.

I got back into the van where Doug was waiting. It seemed huge and grotesquely empty. All kinds of thoughts flooded my mind. Would the girls be all right without me? Kate is, once again, the baby of the family.

How in the world are we going to give our children a happy, carefree childhood? How, for that matter, are we ever going to be happy again? And, boy is this van empty! Nick's car seat was still buckled into the seat directly behind me where I could reach him and hand him his burpie or his juice. But his car seat was empty; empty and yet full of memories of countless car rides. There were drool and juice stains on his car seat straps. Something that he had eaten was spilled on the fabric of the seat. Doug and I looked at one another, took deep breaths, and then he drove us home.

The house, also, was unnaturally quiet as Doug and I went together into Nick's room and sat down on the bottom bunk where our son used to sleep. Our conversation was limited to the idea that we still couldn't believe what had happened. I looked around the room, still completely untouched since the accident. The diaper genie caught my eye and I wondered if there were any diapers in it. I knew I had emptied it before we had left for Clinton, but I thought I remembered changing a dirty diaper right before we left. I lifted the diaper genie and gave it a little shake. I was strangely reassured when I felt the familiar weight and thunk as a diaper hit the side of the container.

In the corner of the room was the coat rack that Grandpa Jay had made for Nick. Several jackets and a baseball cap were hanging on it. I picked up Nick's favorite blue, baseball style jacket. I put it up to my face and took a deep breath. Then I looked into his hood, the thought occurring to me that maybe there would be a little blond hair still stuck inside. There was. I took the hair out and held it up to the light from the window. I felt a deep need to cry. My insides wanted to burst for the emotion that I was feeling, but no tears would come.

Doug was still sitting on the bed, lost in his own thoughts. I showed him the strand of hair and he cried. Not wanting to disturb any of Nick's things, I put the hair as far back in the hood as I could and hung the jacket back on its peg. Then I went to Doug and took his hand and we left Nick's room together. We had one hour to kill before it was time to pick Kate up from preschool.

Later that same day we received a letter in the mail from the Organ Donor Network. It was a listing of the individuals who had received Nick's organs. We were surprised to see four individuals listed as we had previously been told there were only three.

The first to be mentioned was the three-month-old baby girl who had received Nick's heart. She had been waiting two of those three months for a heart and was doing well post-transplant.

Nicholas's liver and small intestine had been transplanted into a two-year-old little girl. She had been waiting for the combined transplant for over a year, and was making slow but positive progress following her surgery.

One of Nick's kidneys was transplanted into a forty-eight-year-old woman and the other into a sixty-four-year-old man. Both were doing well following their transplants. We originally had been told that both of Nick's kidneys had been transplanted into the same adult. Because his kidneys were small, they would work together as one. The letter we received was the first that we had heard that Nick's kidneys had, in fact, gone to two separate people. Someone would tell us later that although, the kidneys were small, they would grow quickly to accommodate the demands placed on them. My only regret in receiving this additional information was that we hadn't been able to tell everyone at the funeral about the fourth person that Nick had been able to help.

I kept myself very busy for the next week or so. I immersed myself in the girls and their activities. The first day back to Allie's dance class one of the mothers asked me where we had been for the past couple of weeks. She was concerned that we had been sick. I told her that we had lost our two-year-old son. She was horrified and covered her mouth uttering, "Oh, God!" She apologized profusely and I assured her that she had asked a legitimate question and shouldn't feel bad. She asked me what had happened and it felt kind of good to talk to her about the accident.

In the evenings, I worked on writing thank-you notes. We were receiving piles of sympathy cards every day in the mail, many of which were from people we didn't even know. Cash and checks came in with the cards and my list of people to thank grew and grew. Doug and I were humbled by the amount of support we were receiving from our friends, family and community. I felt as though I would never be able to thank all of these people appropriately. I took my time with each thank-you card, trying to make my gratitude felt in each word I was writing. If these people only knew how deeply their support was appreciated.

We tried our best to keep our normal routine intact. Kate and I did our thing during the day and by 5:30 each evening, I would have supper ready for when Doug got home from work.

One evening as I was setting the table, Kate came up to me. I could see she was upset and was about to cry. I sat down on one of the kitchen chairs, took her in my lap, and asked her what was wrong. What she said broke my heart. "Mom, I'm sorry I didn't want Nick." And then she started sobbing. I hugged Kate and explained to her that she had nothing to do with Nick's death. In talking with her it came out that she was remembering times when she had told Nick to "go away." In her four-year-old mind, her words had come true, but not in the way that she meant. Now she was feeling responsible. I told her that everyone has times when they are angry and they want someone to go away. We say words we don't really mean, but the whole time that we are mad, we still love the person. Kate stopped crying and I hoped that she understood what I was trying to say to her.

Later that night I could hear Kate talking to herself in the family room. Concerned that she was still feeling guilty about Nick's accident, I peaked around the corner at her. Kate was on her head in the recliner with her feet kicked up over the back of the chair. She was talked to God. I couldn't make out all of what she was saying, but she was telling God that she didn't want Nick to be dead and she wanted God to send him back. It made me feel good that she felt she could talk to God, but sad that she wouldn't understand why her request couldn't be granted.

When the girls were tucked in bed that evening, Doug and I talked to them about how God and all of our loved ones who had already died were watching out for Nick.

He was safe and happy and now would have important things to do helping God. We talked about Nick's organ recipients and how Nick would be taking special care of them. Kate wanted to know if Nick could eat freeze pops and chocolate Pop-tarts whenever he wanted. Not exactly along the same deep lines as what I had been discussing, but her simple question made me smile. I told her I thought he could probably have all the freeze pops and chocolate Pop-tarts that he wanted. We said prayers and kissed the girls good night.

A couple hours later, as I was lying in bed ready to say my own nighttime prayer, I struggled with what I was going to pray. I honestly didn't feel anger at God for Nick's loss, but at the same time, I had prayed so many, many times to God to watch over my family and keep us all safe. Despite my prayers, Nick was gone. I tried to keep the thought "why bother?" out of my head. I know that God didn't take Nick away. Nick had a terrible accident that he couldn't survive. Why Nick wasn't granted a miraculous recovery, I don't know, but I do trust that there was a good reason. I ended up praying my same prayer out of default, but added at the end, "Please watch over Nick. Let him be happy and content." I tried to keep the thought, "Don't let him be missing me the way that I am missing him" out of my head, but I'm sure God heard it anyway. It bothered me to think that Nick was missing us. My hope for him was and is that he continues to love us, but that there is no such feeling as "missing someone" in heaven.

One of the arrangements that still needed to be made was ordering a headstone for Nick's plot at the cemetery.

I had been to the cemetery almost every day, spending a half an hour or so there when Kate was at preschool and I was by myself. There was no marker of any kind to indicate the name of the tiny occupant, but there were always flowers or toys gracing the top of the dirt mound.

One weekend in mid October, Doug and I finally made the appointment to meet with a monument business in Marshalltown. We had made a quick assessment at the cemetery of the color and size of the stone that we wanted. I wrongly assumed that those were the only decisions that we would need to make. Once in the office, however, we were given books to look through containing various types of letters and borders, pictures and epitaphs. The granite came, not only in different sizes and colors, but also in different thicknesses.

Doug and I spent the next hour or so thumbing through the books and making decisions for the monument that would be a tribute to Nick and our family until the end of time. Every once in a while I would lean back in the chair, take a deep breath and get a grip on the fact that this was real. Allison and Kate were being very well behaved and had spent the better part of the past hour roaming the showroom looking nonchalantly at headstones. My heart went out to them that funeral arrangement and things pertaining to death had already become so familiar to them.

In the end, Doug and I felt comfortable with the choices that we had made for our family headstone. Doug's name would appear to the left of Nick's name and my name would appear to the right. Next to Nick's name would be a small picture of a lamb. Under all three of our names would be the words "Together Forever."

During the days that followed, we talked about Nick a lot, reminiscing about all the good times that we had had and remembering all of Nick's funny idiosyncrasies. I worried that, as time went by, the girls would begin to forget things about their brother. We started writing our memories down in a journal and I put together a small photo album with pictures of Nick in it to leave out in the family room. I kept the stuffed animals that Nick had been given in the hospital on our bed, and had searched through the lotion aisle at Wal-Mart to find the lotion that smelled like the one the hospital had used. As the scent started to fade from Nick's little dog, I would put the lotion on my hands and then hold the dog. That way I could smell Nick whenever I needed to.

I became an avid watcher of the John Edwards television program, Crossing Over, watching it as many as three times a day. The program reinforced for me the idea that life does, in fact, go on. I needed to know that Nick was more than okay and that he was still with us in spirit. These were concepts that I already believed, but it was comforting to hear a room-full of other people believing them also.

I admit that I got a little caught up in the pursuit of trying to make sure that our son was safe on the other side. One night after reading one of John Edwards' books, I got the notion to write John Edwards a letter. The final story in his book had been about a young boy who had drowned in a backyard swimming pool. The connection that John had made with this little boy had been very strong. So strong, in fact, that the child was capable of contacting John himself with messages for his family. It occurred to me that maybe Nick could do the same for us.

A concept repeated over and over on Crossing Over is that there are no coincidences. In my mind I was sure that if I could get a letter to John Edwards, he would either hear from Nick or be compelled to contact us. The only address I could find was one to sign up for a newsletter. I thought, well, like the man said, if this is supposed to get to him, it will. Apparently, it wasn't supposed to get to him, because to this date, I haven't heard anything from John Edwards or the Crossing Over program.

I feel a little silly now for writing that letter. It reminds me of when I was ten and I got Harrison Ford's address out of a teen magazine and invited him over for supper. What I didn't realize when I wrote that letter to John Edwards was that I didn't need an outside source to tell me what I needed to know. I was to learn everything that I needed to know from God and Nick themselves.

·

Chapter 4

October 19, 2001, Mom and Dad came to visit for my birthday. I felt comforted seeing them again and yet, at the same time, it was a bittersweet reunion. I had gotten used to my altered environment, seeing the same reminders day after day for the past couple of weeks. But now seeing my parents again brought back a lot of painful memories we had so recently shared together. I think it was hard for them, too, and as we hugged, we all fought to hold back our tears.

Mom had brought with her a stack of sympathy cards, and while Dad and Doug visited and played with the girls, Mom and I sat at the kitchen table and went through them. I was again overwhelmed by the kindness and generosity of so many unknown friends. My list of thank-yous grew, and I was silently glad, knowing that I would have more work to do to occupy my evenings.

Doug and I slept in Nick's bed that night, once again hoping to provide my parents with a squeak-free night's sleep. Before I closed my eyes, I looked around Nick's room. It was fairly dark, the only light coming from the nightlight plugged in near the base of the wall. The light bounced off the wooden potty seat and illuminated the stuffed green dinosaur that Nick had gotten from Don and Linda on his second birthday. I felt strangely at peace lying in Nick's bed, and from the sounds coming from next to me, Doug was already asleep.

I was awakened in the morning by the not so subtle sounds of Doug trying to get out of the bed. I was snug and warm and chose not to say anything. Let him think he had succeeded in getting out of the bed without waking me.

I was very aware of being in Nick's, room and in my half-conscious state, felt my mind reaching out for him. My eyes were still closed and I saw only blackness, but it was as if there was something there in the darkness that I needed to see. And then in the next instant, I did see something. In the upper right corner of my field of vision, set against the blackness of my closed eyes, I saw a splendidly bright American flag. It was there for just a moment and then it was gone. Feeling as though I had been sent some sort of a message, I tried desperately to remain calm so that I could receive more messages. Another image did appear. It was a portion of a photo taken of Nick sitting on Doug's lap. They were riding on the lawn tractor. In this image, however, I only saw Nick's face and the very top part of the navy blue sweatshirt that he had been wearing. As if I were being shown a slide show, that image also vanished and the next picture appeared. I saw the profile of a baby being held in someone's arms. It was being held in a somewhat inclined position and was wearing what appeared to be a Christening gown and bonnet. Part of the gown was obscured by the invisible arm of whoever was holding the child and I was unable to see the baby's face because of the lace edging on the bonnet. As the baby faded from view, I waited for the next slide to appear, but the screen remained black.

The slide show, or as I prefer to think messages from God, had ended. I stayed in bed for another ten minutes trying to interpret what I had seen. If there were any meanings behind the images that I had so vividly viewed in my mind, I couldn't think of what they could be. I felt disappointed in my inability to make sense of what I had been waiting so long to receive. I was also bothered by the picture of Nick. In that photo, although Nick loved riding the tractor with Doug, he had not been smiling. For some reason, when I had taken the picture that day, Nick had had a troubled look on his face. I had to wonder now why that was the image that I saw as opposed to the countless pictures we had of Nick happy and smiling.

Mom and Dad left on Sunday and Doug, the girls and I spent the rest of the day in lazy seclusion. As we were getting the girls ready for bed that night, we heard a lot of commotion coming from the backyard. It sounded to us like a pack of coyotes fighting just off of our back porch. Because it was 8:30 in the evening, it was already dark outside, but all four of us ran to the back patio door and strained to see through the darkness. We saw nothing, but we also didn't hear any more of the eerie snarling and yapping. I went ahead and put the girls to bed, and when I came out from their room, Doug was putting his coat on ready to go out and investigate. Completely out of character for me, as I am normally a total coward, I put my coat on and stepped outside with my husband.

Doug had his big, mega-watt light with him and from a safe position behind him, I helped him scan the backyard for signs of the coyotes. The only things even resembling life were the flannel arms of the scarecrow in our garden as they flapped in the breeze. Guessing that the animals had moved on, Doug turned off the light and we turned to go back into the house. I don't recall who saw them first, but before we could reach the door, we became aware of the most beautiful red northern lights that we had ever seen. We stood, mesmerized by the spectacular sight. Before our eyes, the red streaks seemed to move and undulate with a life of their own. It was several minutes before it occurred to us that we needed to call and tell our parents to look for the lights. Mom, Dad and Marlene were all able to see the lights, but from the descriptions they gave us, it didn't sound like they were quite as brilliant in their areas of the state as compared to what we were seeing.

Having never seen northern lights in Iowa before, Doug and I made the decision that this was something that the girls should see. We went in the house, wrapped their sleepy, jammie clad bodies in blankets and brought them outside with us. They were impressed, but I think, spoiled from a life-time of movie special effects, not quite as wowed by the magnificence of nature's beauty as Doug and I were. Five minutes later they were snug and cozy back in their beds.

Doug and I had private conversation that night as to the significance we believed to be behind the lights, and to the circumstances that had taken both of us outside into the night to see them. It wasn't until the next day, however, that it hit me. I called Doug at work, and had difficulty talking through my tears. "Doug, yesterday was my birthday!" I had been given a precious and spectacular birthday present, direct from heaven and my little boy.

The next big hurdle I was to encounter was Halloween. Allison and Kate were very excited, and sticking to my vow to keep life normal for them, we went about preparations for the upcoming holiday. I felt guilty about my lack of enthusiasm, feeling as if I were only going through the motions for them. I would much rather have been there for them heart, body and soul, but instead I felt as if I were only giving them body. I did the best that I could, however.

We dug the decorations out of the attic and went shopping for costumes. Both girls chose to be witches; not the scary kind, but the cute kind with bright orange and purple glitter decorating their dresses and pointy hats. We bought pumpkins and carved them. Well, not "we" exactly. Doug carved pumpkins with them. I opted to be the photographer, mostly to hide the tears that kept appearing in my eyes. Thoughts of the previous Halloween haunted me with visions of Nick standing amid the giant pumpkins at the pumpkin farm, and Nick dressed up in his Alligator costume, although he wouldn't leave the head on because it kept falling over his eyes. I was remembering how much fun he had had his first time Trick-or-Treating.

This year when we took the girls Trick-or-Treating, we all went together. I, personally, had no desire to go with my family, but went anyway so that the girls would see me as participating and sharing in their fun. We went to the homes of some of our former neighbors, but due to the rain and cold, we ended up at the middle school. One of the local churches hosted a Fall Festival on Trick-or-Treat night. The years that the weather was bad, it was a real blessing. The kids could play games, win candy, visit with their friends, and generally, have a very good time. The parents from the community also had a chance to visit. This year, however, visiting was more than I could handle.

Once inside the school's gymnasium we found an inconspicuous place to stand and were talking with our friends Wayne and Jana. Another couple came to join us, and for the moment, I found myself out of the immediate conversation. Looking around I saw Kate playing a game near us and Allie was with a friend playing the beanbag toss. I saw many people I knew, but some that I didn't. A couple that I didn't recognize had just come through the door. With them was a small boy maybe two or three years old. He was wearing footy pajamas and he had a very familiar blond hair cut. All of the strength and composure that I had been fighting all night to keep under control left me. I touched Doug's arm and he immediately turned from his conversation to look at me. I was already wiping at the tears that had started to roll down my cheeks. "I'm going to go out to the car." I whispered this to him, trying not to draw attention to myself. He handed me the keys with a knowing look, and said he'd round up the girls and meet me out there. I felt bad that the girls would leave early on my account and told him not to hurry. Some time to myself would do me good.

I wasn't able to get across the entire gymnasium without being noticed and had collected quite a few hugs by the time I reached the door. It was pitch black and raining quite hard as I tried to find the van amid the sea of cars in the parking lot. I was glad for the darkness, the rain and the cool night air on my face. I hadn't realized what an effort I had been making to hold myself together throughout the evening. I found the van, sat in the front passenger seat and had myself a good cry. I still found it hard to cry, but when I did, it felt really good.

I had been in the van only a few minutes when I heard a tapping on the window. Startled, I wiped at the condensation I had created and saw my friend Donna looking in at me. She obviously had seen me leave and confirmed my suspicion once the door was open. I scooted over into the driver's seat and Donna took the seat I had vacated.

Donna had convinced me to share a job with her the year before as an aide for a child at the middle school. She had taken mornings and I had taken afternoons. Part of our arrangement was that I would watch her kids while she worked and she would watch my kids while I worked. In the process we had grown very attached to one another's children and the kids in turn had become fast friends.

So now, sitting in the dark with rain streaking down the windows, Donna and I reminisced about our babysitting days and had a deep discussion about death and faith. We both cried and when Doug and the girls came running to the van, I felt as though the talk that Donna and I had shared had done me some good. We hugged, promised not to be such strangers and said goodbye. Then my husband, our two little witches, and I headed for home. I had survived Halloween. Now I just had to get through the rest of my life.

On November 3, 2001, my parents, Marlene, my Aunt Colette and cousin Meg came to our house once again so that they would be there to attend the benefit given in honor of Nicholas by the community. Several friends had approached us with the suggestion of having a benefit. Our first reaction was to humbly decline the offer. We felt that our friends and the community had done more than enough already, and to accept more just didn't seem right. Doug and I told them as much, but the reply that we received was reminiscent of the statement that my mom had made when I had told her about the idea for a benefit. Simply put, people had empathy for and cared about us. I think a tragedy had hit very close to home for those around us and they felt a need to do something about it. The benefit, apparently, was a way that they felt they could help our family. Reluctantly, we agreed.

The benefit was held at the Dakin's Center in Zearing. Inside the door, sitting at a card table were our pastor's wife, Rachel, and Donna. They were taking donations in a basket that was surrounded by pictures of Nick. To the left of them were tables of baked goods and items that had been donated for auctioning (all organized and mostly donated by Shawn and the bar that she and her husband owned). To the right of the donation table was the kitchen. Inside were numerous women and men from our church and the town's nurse practitioner, Dr. Mary. They were serving the food; BBQ pork sandwiches, baked beans, salads and bars. All had been donated or purchased for a fraction of the cost.

To say that I felt inadequate to thank everyone for all they were doing was an understatement. In fact, I was regretting my decision to come altogether. Our friends had told us that we weren't expected to be there, that given the circumstances, people would understand if it would be too difficult for us to attend. Doug and I, however, felt that we should be there, if for no other reason than to show the community that we appreciated what they were doing for us. Standing in that room, seeing our friends and community family, all there working…all for us, was quite overwhelming. I remember stepping back outside for a moment to catch my breath. Dad was out there, too, apparently feeling a need for some air as well. He was talking with Allie's bus driver and former co-worker of mine from the middle school. They were having some everyday, normal conversation and after a deep breath and a hug from my dad, I was ready to go back inside.

Doug and the rest of our family were still in the front room. They had been looking over the baked goods and auction items, and I think, maybe, were waiting for me to rejoin them. We passed by the donation table to enter the dining area and I had to fight the urge to put money into the basket. I think my mom sensed my uneasiness, and from behind me whispered in my ear, "I'll put in enough for all of you, too." Thanks, Mom.

As we stood there in the food line, I felt so thankful for the love and support of my family behind me. And I don't just mean the ones who were able to attend the benefit. Doug's family and my family had always been there for us, through the good times and the bad. And then there was Doug himself. His hand was always there on my back, making his presence known and always giving me the reassurance and support that I needed from him. Now, entering the community center dining room, I was so thankful for them all and so deeply sorry that they had to go through this with me.

The girls, who had located friends, were happily playing some sort of chasing game up near the stage. It occurred to me to tell them to stop running and talk more quietly, but then I changed my mind. Let them have their fun. They were good girls, considerate and polite most of the time. They would be fine.

Doug and I each picked up two plates, one for us and the other for Allie or Kate. Eventually, we figured, the girls would tire out, get hungry, or their friends would have to leave. So now, we not only hadn't paid for our supper, but we were each carrying two plates! As we passed through the line, being served by our friends from church, we thanked them each sincerely for their participation with the benefit.

With our meals in hand, we scanned the room for a place to sit. Most people we recognized, but there were man that I don't recall ever having seen before. I thought of all the times that I hadn't attended a benefit for the simple reason that I didn't know the people involved. I felt ashamed of myself and decided to try to be better about my attendance in the future.

We found places to sit near the back of the room. Doug and I were touched to see some former neighbors of ours from Slater. We hadn't seen them for several years, and now we were seeing them again for the second time in less than two months. They, and several of our friends from Slater, had been at the church the night of Nick's visitation. It was the first time that they had, in fact, ever seen Nick.

We sat down with our old friends, and although they were finished eating, they stayed with us and we caught up on all the latest news from Slater. The rest of our family members had chosen to sit at other tables, and as I looked around for them, I was happy to see that they had found people to visit with.

Eventually, the girls found a moment and came over to our table to eat their cold suppers. Many friends and neighbors had stopped by our table throughout the course of the evening, and when we were ready to leave, we didn't feel obligated to stop at each table to tell everyone thank you.

Before we could exit the building, the female members of my family stopped to purchase some of the baked goods still sitting out on the tables. I happened to see the price tag on the loaf of homemade white bread that my aunt was holding. I thought to myself that I would owe her homemade white bread for a very long time. Not only did my aunt buy a very costly loaf of bread, but she also put in a bid on one of the auction items, a lamp in the shape of a giant light bulb. Whether she really wanted a giant light bulb shaped lamp, I don't know, but she did end up being the lucky bidder to take it home.

Nick's bedroom and possessions had remained untouched up until this point. Doug and I had been discussing moving the girls down from upstairs. We weren't comfortable with them sleeping upstairs by themselves given the age of the wiring in the house. It was a difficult decision for us, but we concluded that, for safety's sake, we would move the girls into Nick's room downstairs.

Before we touched any of Nick's things, we took pictures of everything in the room, including the miniature baseball and baseball glove hanging from the ceiling fan pulls. The bed, which had been slept in when we had had company had been neatly remade. Wanting everything to look as if Nick had just left the room, I pulled down the comforter and replaced Nick's drool-stained pillow where our pillows had been. I lay his two-piece, blue and white blanket sleeper and his blue socks next to the pillow where I was accustomed to putting them after dressing him each morning. I was disappointed that all of Nick's burpies had been laundered. I had created an authentic scene except for the presence of a well-used burpie. On impulse, I checked between the bed and the wall, pulling aside the primary colored plaid comforter and the coordinating red bed skirt. Guided by some unknown force, I kept up my search. I was rewarded momentarily by the familiar feel of one of the well-worn cloths. I remember shaking my head as if I knew that my need had been fulfilled by a small, loving boy trying to sooth his distraught mother. "Here, Mommy," I could almost hear him say. I placed Nick's burpie, still smelling of him, next to his jammies. I felt a tremendous sense of relief. His room was now truly returned to the way that he had left it.

Realistically I knew that it would be impossible to keep Nick's room, and our house in general, as it had been before the accident, but at least we would have these pictures. Some day when our memories had faded, we would pull out the pictures and we would be reminded of all the details that we had forgotten. "Remember how Nick used to love to play that little Sesame Street saxophone? See, there it is on his toy shelf. Oh, and there's the cross necklace the Allie made for him. I'd almost forgotten about that."

In preparation for the move, I took Nick's clothes out of the closet. Anything that Nick had never worn or that I had no particular fondness for, I put in a pile to be given away. Everything else was meticulously folded and placed with care in his dresser.

I did the same with the toys, keeping anything with a memory attached to it and getting rid of the toys that would just be taking up space. Nick's dresser and toy box were filled to capacity by the time I was finished, and they contained precious memories that I planned to keep for as long as I lived.

Doug and I carried Nick's dresser and toy box to our upstairs storage room that night. I returned the Winnie the Pooh nightlight and wipe container to their rightful places on the top of the dresser and made sure that nothing else would be blocking entrance to either the dresser or toy box. I wanted to be able to open them whenever I needed to.

I felt a certain sense of betrayal as I turned the light off and left the room. As I did so often, I whispered out loud to Nick that no matter what changes were made in our family, he would never be replaced or forgotten. I prayed that he knew this and I really felt that he could feel our love and commitment to him across the boundaries of life and death.

It was the certainty that Nick was still deeply connected to our family that had allowed me to press forward and be "okay" up until this point. I had to trust that God would continue to give me the strength I needed to get through the days to come in a quality way. The biggest fear that I had these days, besides the safety for the rest of my family, was the fear of losing my faith. I knew that if I could not believe that Nick was in the best of hands with God, that I would not be able to cope with the tragedy that had befallen him. I would be unable to function as a capable wife, mother, and daughter, and I would be destroyed.

Nick's room may not have looked like Nick's room anymore, but there were reminders everywhere of our son and what could and should have been. One of our first ventures back into public was to Burger King. Leaving the house, I kept feeling as though I were forgetting something. I hesitated before I closed the door behind me, going through in my mind that I had my purse, money and our shopping list. Then it dawned on me that it was the diaper bag that I was missing. It was so ingrained in Doug and me to grab the diaper bag that it felt wrong not to have it on my arm now.

Once at Burger King, we were again in for another blast of our new reality. We fought the urge to order three kid's meals, one with a toddler toy. Then, once we had finished eating, it tore out our hearts to watch the girls playing "alone" on the play equipment. Although they never said anything, I could see the sideways glances they made at the small boys playing near them. I could sense their thoughts, their loss, and was very glad when it was time for us to leave.

We did our shopping and decided to end the afternoon at the movie theater. We found our seats, had our popcorn and drinks in hand and were eagerly awaiting the show when another family came and sat in the vacant seats next to Doug. It was a young couple and their small boy, approximately the same age as Nick, and, of course, he was blond. For some unknown reason the child would not stop staring at Doug.

It was the oddest sensation to have this boy continue looking at Doug so intently. My heart went out to my husband, both of us feeling the discomfort of the situation. We exchanged tear-glazed glances at one another that plead the question "What do we do?" The child's parents seemed oblivious to their child's interest in Doug and after an eternity of painfully forced smiles at the boy, the light went off in the theater and the previews started.

Another Saturday found us sitting in Taco Johns waiting for our name to be called so that we could pick up our order. Four college boys came in and sat down at a booth across the aisle from us. One of the boys looked "familiar" and I caught myself staring at him. If I tried to predict what Nick would have looked like at that age, this boy would pretty much have matched the image in my mind. Our name was eventually called and I did my best to turn my attention back to my family and the burrito in front of me. I managed very well until I heard "Nicholas" called from the pick-up counter. The boy that I had noticed got up and went to pick up his food. I finished yet another meal trying hard to swallow despite the large lump in my throat.

Visual reminders were everywhere and, all of a sudden, so were the stories of other mothers who had lost children. I suppose I hadn't paid attention to all of the women around me who had suffered a loss such as mine. Perhaps I didn't pay attention for the simple reason that I never wanted to share in what it must feel like to walk in their shoes. I was like many other parents who found the thought of losing a child so painful that I refused to even consider the possibility. Kind of like when I was pregnant for the first time and was reading childbirth books. I would never read the parts about C-sections. The thought of having a C-section scared me, so I didn't want to read about them. Of course, I ended up having one.

In visiting with other mothers who had lost children, I learned how sensitive and even possessive I was when it came to discussing Nick's death. I didn't want to hear how the other mothers' children had died. I felt like I was being asked to judge which mother's circumstances had been the most painful. I had been told by a mother who had lost her son in his 40's, that at least I only had two years of memories to miss. I felt like saying, "You should be thankful that your son had so many years to make memories. And by the way, when was the last time your son climbed in bed with you in the morning?" Another mother would say to me of her two grown sons, "At least you only lost one son. I lost two." Oddly enough, her losing two sons didn't seem to diminish any of the pain that I was feeling for losing Nick. I know that both women were trying to lend me support because they knew what it felt like to experience a child's death. Perhaps I was being overly sensitive, but I felt like they were telling me that I didn't have it as bad as they did.

I planned to learn from these situations and remember that another's pain and loss are relative only to the pain and loss that he or she has already experienced. The whole concept is extremely personal and cannot be compared to what someone else may or may not have experienced.

I wished that Allie's and Kate's only experiences with pain and loss could have been breaking up with a bad boyfriend. It hurt me to think that, at their early ages, they already had their pain scales set high having tragically lost a brother. I prayed for them that they would never have to endure a pain like that again.

In an effort to get back into our normal routine, we started going to church again. I couldn't bring myself to attend the first few Sundays, partly because I felt like we would be pitied and we would have to answer hundreds of questions about how we were doing. I knew I would have a hard enough time handling the multitude of feelings that I would inevitably experience. My eyes would be drawn to the two spots where Nick's casket had sat and I would relive the day of his funeral over and over again in my mind. Cause enough for procrastination in my book. But I also knew that the longer I stayed away from church, the harder it would be for me to go back.

So we went back to church, getting there early so we could get a pew in the back. Not that our church was always packed full of people. Being a town of less than 700 residents, Zearing was home to four separate churches. Despite the diminutive size of the Methodist congregation, the back pews were always highly sought after and would eventually seat the majority of the congregation by the time Pastor Lynn made his way to the pulpit. I used to find the seating arrangement kind of comical. It was as if congregation members expected the "Wrath of God" to shoot through the pastor's eyes or something. Actually, the back pews were mostly filled by those of us with young children. Sitting in the back enabled us to be able to sneak out should the natives grow restless.

My thoughts took a different course this time, and instead of sitting in the back of the sanctuary because of the kids and their noise potential, we sat in the back for a whole new set of reasons. We chose our seats on the very outside edge of the last pew; hiding perhaps or enabling a quick escape, I'm not really sure.

I was proud of my behavior in church that day, although I did cry through all the hymns. I did well that is until the sermon. The content of the sermon is a little foggy to me now, but I do remember what thoughts were running through my head as I listened to Pastor Lynn speak. He was talking about how, in the Bible, God tells us to follow the example given to us by Jesus. We should dedicate ourselves to doing God's work and in return, all of our needs would be met. We would be protected, taken care of, and provided for.

As I looked over the heads of the people in front of me, some of them nodding in agreement to the words of the sermon, I became very angry. I replayed in my mind images of Nick lying in bed at night with his hands folded and proudly saying the prayer that he had memorized. I saw Nick reaching his hand out to the elderly and handicapped as though he knew how much his smile and touch would mean to them. I saw Nick carrying around his sisters' baby dolls, handling them with tenderness and care. And I felt the tremendous love from him as he put his arms around my neck and gave me a kiss. If this wasn't a parishioner doing his best to follow in the footsteps of Christ, then who was? If righteous qualities are what God wants from us, then why had he allowed the loss of one of his best? Nick was just getting started in life. He could have done so much good.

I did feel anger at God, and the whole congregation, at that moment. I watched everyone bow their heads and pray to the God who had not protected, but who, in fact, had allowed the death of an individual who was doing everything right.

I was the first one out of church that day, afraid that I would not be able to keep the contempt that I was feeling out of my eyes and voice. Once we were in the van I told Doug why I had made such a speedy exit. Saying the words, I could hear my bitterness and knew that I had entered the "anger" phase of my grieving. Thankfully, I needed God too much to be angry for long, and by the time we had reached home, I had come to the conclusion that maybe it was because Nick was so pure and good that God needed him. There was no way for me to know God's plan, but I needed to trust that it was a really good one. There is that saying that God only takes the best. It's comforting to think that there may be something to those words because the alternative is incomprehensible, that there was no reason for Nick's death.

I believe with everything in me that Nick's drowning was just an accident. God didn't want or cause Nick to fall into the pond. As for the reason that Nick didn't recover from his accident? Now that is the big question. It wasn't for lack of love, faith, or prayers. More likely it was because of some virtue that Nick possessed. Oddly enough, I was able to feel very proud of Nick, for saving lives through organ donation, but also for the very special something that he possessed and that God saw and needed.

By the end of November, cards gradually ceased coming in the mail, so it was a nice surprise when I took the mail out of the box one afternoon and saw a card from Nick's nurse, Amy.

Amy, we had learned, had spent a lot of time with Nick after we had left the hospital for home. She had talked to Nick, kissed him, and later had gone with him for the organ retrieval surgery. In the end Amy had dressed Nick in the jeans and long sleeved tan t-shirt that I had left for him. Instead of allowing Nick to be taken out of the OR on a gurney, Amy had carried him in her arms.

I knew that God had created very special people to work in the Pediatric Intensive Care Unit with those critically ill children, but I would never be able to appropriately convey to Amy my gratitude for doing what I could not do myself. She came to work to do her job, but went above and beyond her duty as a PICU nurse by displaying such tremendous caring and compassion.

Holding Amy's card in my hand, images of her spending those last precious minutes with our son filled my mind, and it was with trembling hands that I opened her correspondence. Inside the envelope was a beautiful, embossed card, but it was the contents of the card that had my attention. There, inside, was a lock of silky, blond hair. It had at one time been tied together by a little black string. I put the Ziploc containing Nick's lock of hair to my lips and cried. I wanted to open the bag and feel the familiar silkiness, but was afraid that by doing so, the lock would completely fall apart.

I dried my tears enough so that I could read Amy's small, neat handwriting. She apologized for having taken so long to get Nick's lock of hair to us, and for the fact that the string had not stayed in place. She explained that she had been carrying Nick's hair around with her in her purse and had found it hard to part with. She said that she knew that any part of Nick would be precious to us, but she hoped that receiving the lock wouldn't be too hard. She was right on both counts. Receiving Nick's lock of hair made me long for him with a ferocity that is indescribable. And yet for a person who had saved her son's poopy diaper, smelled his shoes, and caressed a drool spot on a pillowcase, it was a tremendously sacred gift. I called Doug immediately, and then sat down and wrote Amy a letter that I hoped would in some way convey to her our gratitude for all that she had done.

It wasn't long after the arrival of Amy's letter that we received a package from the PICU at the hospital in Iowa City. The box contained three very carefully wrapped plates. On each plate was a beautifully painted handprint. I vaguely recalled the nurses taking the plaster imprints of Nick's lifeless little hands the night before he was declared brain dead. Each plate had been painstakingly painted; one was yellow with the alphabet printed around the edge in primary colors, one was light blue with yellow stars, and one was navy blue with yellow dots around the edge. This last one, although it had been chipped in the mail, was the one that we chose to keep for ourselves. It was the only plate of the three to have both a hand and a footprint. All three plates had "Nicholas" printed above the handprint and all three had the wrong birth date written below.

I felt sick looking at those wrong dates on the otherwise perfectly crafted memorials. It was my fault that the date was wrong. When Nick had first arrived at the hospital in Clinton following his accident, someone had asked me for Nick's personal information. I remember feeling like I couldn't think. I couldn't remember even the most basic facts, such as our address and phone number. I was the one who told them that Nick's birthday was June 19 instead of the actual date of June 17. Kate's birthday was the 19th of January and I think that is where the 19 came from.

Later on we would give the light blue handprint to Marlene and the yellow handprint to Mom and Dad. Dad, who could fix anything and solve any dilemma, took a pocket-knife and turned their 19 into a 17 without disturbing any of the paint underneath. I toyed with doing the same to our plate, but decided that the mistake had a lot of significance behind it. Doug and I were likely to be the only ones to ever notice the discrepancy and we would always remember what it had felt like that night in the hospital when the only thing filling our minds were prayers for our son's recovery.

Knowing that we would be going to Clinton for Thanksgiving, our first visit since the accident, I felt the need to go home one week-end before then by myself. I wasn't sure what my reaction would be when I went to the backyard and saw the pond again, but I was reasonably certain that it would be best if the girls weren't with me.

Approximately five miles from the house, I started shaking and sobbing uncontrollably anticipating what it was going to be like to revisit the location where we had lost our child. On my trip to Clinton, I had passed crosses carefully placed along the roadside indicating the location where a loved one had been lost. I was silently grateful that I had a beautiful and secluded place to honor Nick's passing. But as I got closer to home, I was also saddened that I would never be able to go home again without having to relive that fateful day. My heart went out to my parents as well. They would be reminded daily.

Mom and Dad had asked Doug and me what we wanted to do about the pond. They were willing to fill the pond in, but even if the pond were gone from sight, the location and memory of what had happened would always be with us. Besides, Nick loved that pond. It was beautiful and the kids had always enjoyed feeding and watching the goldfish that swam within it. We had concluded, as a family, that the pond would be left alone.

Pulling into my parents' driveway, I was glad, for the first time, not to have a greeting committee. I needed to be alone and I was sure that Mom and Dad knew that, so had not come out to greet me on purpose.

I took a deep breath and rounded the house to the backyard. My eyes went directly to the sidewalk as that was the last place that I had seen Nick, before I knew exactly what had happened. In my memory I could see him lying with his head down in the grass in an attempt to keep his airway open for rescue breathing. The rest of his body had been placed, so pale and still, up on the sidewalk. I could see the dampness left on the cement after the ambulance had taken him to the hospital, and I could see his clothes and shoes strewn around by the paramedics.

I stopped just short of that significant patch of sidewalk, remembering every detail with a clarity that was frightening. Then I turned in place and looked upon the path through the flowers that our son must have taken when he went up to the pond that last day.

I saw the rosebush; little more than a stick, that had miraculously given birth to one tiny, but perfect, miniature pink rose the day after Nick's accident. I retraced Nick's footsteps to the edge of the pond then knelt down and did what came naturally to me. I put one hand in the water and held it there. The water was so cold. Under normal circumstances, I would have pulled my hand out immediately, but this wasn't a normal circumstance and I felt a need to share, in part, what Nick must have felt.

I didn't sob as I thought I would and yet tears were silently coursing down my face. I thought again that God was merciful and he would have snatched Nick up to heaven before he even had a chance to feel the iciness of the water. I desperately had to believe that Nick didn't suffer.

I'm not sure how long I stayed there with my hand in the pond, but after another deep breath I felt a sense of relief as though I had conquered some unknown foe. As I stood up I looked down at my hand. It was red from being submersed in the icy water. I didn't dry my hand on my jeans, but instead put my moistened hand to my lips. I felt the water on my lips and was aware that I had listened to the same water gurgling in Nick's lungs when we had breathed air into him.

When I was ready, I went to the back patio door expecting to yell up the stairs at my parents, "Hi, I'm here!" But when I reached the door, I could see them standing back a ways, holding one another. They obviously knew that I was home and from their expressions had just witnessed my return to the pond. They came forward as one and we all hugged. No words had been spoken, but none were necessary as my mom and dad held me tight and we sobbed into one another's shoulders.

My visit was healing in that I was able to focus on myself and my own feelings at the scene of Nick's accident. When I left to go home to Zearing two days later, I felt strengthened. I hoped that, on my next trip "home," I would be able to be a source of comfort for my husband and children as my parents had been for me.

Thanksgiving arrived and I was again on my way home to Clinton, this time with my family. I was relieved to have gotten my first visit over with, but felt badly that Doug and the girls had yet to have theirs. We pulled into the driveway and were met shortly thereafter by Mom and Dad. Hugs all around and then we went into the house by way of the garage. No one said anything, but I think it was understood that Doug would want to be alone if and when he was ready to revisit the pond.

Eric and Vickie were already inside and Allison and Kate were soon playing with their cousin David. It was good to be back with family, celebrating a holiday that we could associate with good times and loved ones. Our conversation stayed mostly to safe topics, no one wanting to reminisce too deeply into our recent tragedy.

That night as Doug and I pulled out the sofa bed and were putting on the sheets, I remembered the night a few months previously when I had made a cozy little nest on the sofa bed for Nick. Over in the corner was the miniature Harley that the grandkids took turns riding whenever they were visiting Grandpa and Grandma. A child size black, Harley baseball cap was hanging on one of the handlebars. That hat brought to mind some recent pictures that we had taken of Nick. He had been wearing the hat backwards, as was his custom, and he was sitting proudly upon the little motorcycle. We had all laughed at Nick, telling him how handsome he looked, and he had reveled in the attention from his admirers.

I did sleep well that night, at least as well as one can on a sofa bed mattress, until 5:30 AM the next morning. I awoke with tears in my eyes, not sad tears, but tears of overwhelming relief and gratitude. I say that I had a dream, but I'm not sure that is the appropriate term. Maybe a "visit" is more accurate.

In my "dream" I was entering a house. I came into a dining room and sitting in one of the dining table chairs facing me was Doug's dad, Jay. I knew that he had passed away, so I felt shock and surprise at seeing him. He looked really good, like he had looked before he had gotten sick with cancer. He put his arms out to me and said, "Do you have a hug for an old man?" I started to cry and walked into his outstretched arms. He lifted me up above his head with straight arms, like one would lift a small child. I could feel his strength and vitality. He was no longer the thin, weakened man that we had watched pass away in a hospice a year previously.

As Jay brought me back down, I turned my face into

his neck thinking I would smell the familiar cologne that he often wore. I was vaguely aware that I didn't detect any smells at all, but soon forgot about odors as I looked into the eyes of my father-in-law. Jay had big, beautiful brown eyes, just like Doug's, but the eyes that I was looking into were bright blue and were too small for the sockets that I was seeing. In some remote part of my brain, the discrepancy registered, but I wouldn't think much about those eyes until much later.

For now, I had one thing on my mind, and that was to find out as much as I could about Nick.

I was still standing directly in front of Jay when I asked him the first question. "Is Nick okay?"

Jay smiled gently at me and said, "Nick is just fine." Not wanting to waste precious moments I asked the next question.

"Is Nick happy?"

Jay gestured to his left and said, "He's standing right over there and he's smiling." I looked in the direction that Jay was pointing, but all I could see was a built-in wooden colonnade similar to the one in Jay and Marlene's house in Northwood.

Next I asked him, "What was he doing?" This said with sad desperation. Jay didn't answer me right away, but rather turned to where he said that Nick was standing. It was as if Jay were being told by Nick what he had been doing when he had fallen into the pond.

Jay was still looking in Nick's direction when he answered me. "I was reaching for a (plane?)"... and then something about tripping and falling.

That part has remained frustratingly vague because at that moment I heard footsteps on the kitchen floor above me and I was waking up.

Afraid that I would forget even the tiniest detail, I turned to Doug and shook his shoulder gently until he woke up. Then I relayed to him all that I had seen and heard.

I felt so blessed to have received this message because so many of the questions that I really felt I needed answered had been, for the most part, answered. I had confirmed that Nick was okay and was able to "enjoy". I also confirmed my suspicion that Nick had been reaching for something and had lost his footing thereby falling into the pond. I also had one question indirectly answered that had been bothering me. I believed that our loved ones who had passed away had the ability to watch over those of us still on Earth. So I had struggled with the question of why Jay hadn't been able to do anything to prevent Nick's accident. How hard could it have been to signal Doug and Dad to turn in time to see Nick near the pond?

My question had been answered when Jay had to turn to Nick to find out what he was doing at the moment of his accident. Jay had to ask because at that particular moment, he hadn't "been there," so couldn't have stopped events from unfolding. It was as if Jay knew Nick was in heaven with him, but didn't know how he had gotten there.

I was deeply relieved and thankful that Doug genuinely believed in the messages of my dream. There was no doubt or skepticism in his eyes and I think that perhaps he needed this dream as much as I did. We made the decision to tell the rest of the family about my dream in the hopes that they would be comforted as we had been. And they were.

Later as I thought about Jay's eyes, I had to wonder if they weren't actually Jay's eyes at all, but were, instead, Nick's. I know that if I had seen Nick in my dream, I wouldn't have been able to listen to a word. I would have been frantically trying to seek a way to grab hold of Nick and pull him back to me. So did I see Jay or Nick in the image of Jay? Did God know that I wasn't ready to see Nick yet? These are questions that remain and that I may never know the answers to, but that's okay. I did receive answers that I really needed. I needed to know that Nick is happy and with his grandpa and loved ones in heaven. And I also needed to know that Jay couldn't have done anything to help Nick.

Chapter 5

Shortly after Thanksgiving, I decided that it was time to write the first letters to Nick's organ recipients. I felt a deep curiosity as to who these people were and I was desperate to hear that our decision to donate Nick's organs had had successful results. I had already put Nick up on a high pedestal as a hero who had saved the lives of others. Now I wanted the proof, and I admit, I wanted the recognition for Nick that he had done this wonderful thing. I wanted a chance to tell the recipients who Nick was and I wanted to send them pictures, so at night when they were lying in bed, it would be Nick's precious little face that they would see and feel blessed by.

Sometimes I feel vain for wanting the whole world to know who Nick was and what he did through organ donation. I should be content, perhaps, that God and our friends and family know of his tremendous gifts to four suffering souls. But if I had a way of making the whole world be proud of Nick as we are...if I could set Nick up as a model for others on how to live compassionately, show them the healing power of knowing that a loved one left this world having made the lives of others better, what a wonderful tribute to Nick that would be.

So, with these thoughts in mind, I sat down and wrote four identical letters to Nick's recipients:

> Dear Recipient and Family,
> We wanted to let you know that we are thinking of you and are praying for you to make a complete recovery with your transplant. Our greatest hope is that you will live a long, happy and quality life and that you will bring lots of love to those around you. Just know that you have a family in Iowa who is comforted by you, who cares for you deeply, and who is praying for you daily.
> Your donor family,
> Doug, Erin, Allison, and Kate

I wanted to include photos and information about Nick, but had been warned by the Organ Donor Network (ODN) that it could be difficult for recipients to receive correspondence from their donor families. Recipients and their families lived with knowing that they hoped and prayed for a suitable organ but at the cost of another life.

I wanted to be sensitive to those feelings, although in doing so I was delaying my own need for contact with these people. As it was, it would be several weeks before my letter would find its way through the appropriate channels and into the hands of the recipients.

I was repeatedly frustrated by the system of correspondence. Confidentiality was the name of the game. I wrote a letter and put it in an unmarked envelope with a sticky note attached. On the sticky note was the name of the recipient the letter was addressed to, and Nick's name and date of death. I put the unsealed envelope inside another envelope and addressed it to the family services department at the ODN. Once my letter was received at the ODN, they read the letter, checking it for any information that could compromise confidentiality, put my letter in another envelope and addressed it to the transplant hospital for the appropriate individual. A week or so later, I would get a letter from the ODN containing the date that my "treasured correspondence" was mailed.

Even if the recipient family were to respond the same day as they had received my letter, I could count on not hearing anything back for a month or more from the date I sent my letter. Despite knowing the length of the process, I picked up the mail every day, always hopeful that there would be a letter from one of the recipients in the box. And every day I was disappointed.

On December 8, 2001, we were invited to attend an open house at the State Capitol Building in Des Moines. Governor Tom Vilsack and First Lady Christie Vilsack would be in attendance to honor all of those who had given the gift of life through organ donation. Doug and I had struggled with whether or not we were ready to attend such an event, but in the end decided that going to the open house would be a way that we could honor Nick and tell his story.

Walking into the Capitol building, I wanted many times to turn around and leave. When I saw the hundreds of people visiting and mingling just inside the entrance, my feelings intensified and at one point, Doug and I did actually turn around and head for the door. But then my thoughts turned to Nick and a new determination came over me. This was something that I could do for him.

We followed the sign that led us to a large room downstairs. Card tables were set up, one for each letter of the alphabet. We got in the "H" line and waited to be handed Nick's certificate. Inside a navy blue folder, stamped with the seal of Iowa, was an ivory certificate that read, "An offering of gratitude to honor Nicholas Hulshizer who gave the hope for tomorrow." Governor Vilsack's and Lt. Governor Pederson's signatures were written on the bottom of the certificate.

Whether with pride or with sorrow, my eyes filled with tears. Doug and I went to regroup in a hallway just off of the main room. It was while we were standing there trying to get our emotions under control that we first saw Amney.

The last time we had seen Amney had been at the hospital in Iowa City. As a representative for the ODN, Amney had been the one to go over the procedure with us for organ donation. The memory of sitting in a conference room with her and answering health related and personal questions about our two-year-old son came flooding back into our memories. Had Nick ever taken any illegal drugs? Had he ever engaged in sexual intercourse with multiple partners? Amney apologized for having to ask questions that obviously didn't apply to a two-year-old, but explained that she had to ask us every question on the form.

Amney had done an excellent job that day of

compassionately telling us what we needed to know. She hadn't pressured or coerced us on the subject of donating Nick's organs. She had merely presented us with the facts. Amney had been sympathetic to our situation and we were left to make our own decisions based on the information we were given. We had respected Amney and the organ donor program for their sensitivity. Seeing her across the room, however, obviously reminiscing with some other families, I wasn't sure if I wanted to go up to her and give her a big hug or avoid revisiting more painful memories and try to escape the room without being noticed. Doug and I decided, for the moment, that we would pretend that we hadn't seen her.

With a photo of Nick and now his certificate in my hands, the four of us climbed the steps to the main level. We were again stunned by what must have been several hundred people. I felt overwhelmed and clutched Nick's picture tightly to my chest feeling a need to protect him.

People were everywhere; standing in groups, laughing and talking together, waiting in lines to view the memory quilts and standing around tables to look at literature. There were tables of refreshments and tables selling ODN items like greeting cards and pins. Towards the back of the vast room there appeared to be another very large and slow moving line. It wasn't a "stand behind the person in front of you" line. It was more of a creeping mass of heads that was as wide as the hallway and filtered through a single door at the end. We figured that must be the line you survived to see the governor.

Standing there observing the sights and sounds surrounding me, I suddenly felt very claustrophobic and wanted nothing else but to walk out the door we had come in, get in our van, and drive away. I told Doug I didn't think I could stay any longer, so with Allie and Kate in tow, we headed back the way we had come. As we approached the doors that led down the front of the capital building, I felt unwelcome waves of guilt. Nick's picture was still pressed to my chest and, as I thought of him, I felt like I would be betraying him by leaving. It was very painful and difficult for Doug and I to stay in an environment that brought back such vivid memories of a time we wanted to erase, but we hadn't come to the Capitol for us, we had come for Nick.

With that realization, I told Doug that I had changed my mind and that I wanted to stay and stand in that wretched line, because in the end, we would know that we had done something for our son. With renewed determination I vowed to stay at the open house until I had showed Governor Vilsack Nick's picture and told him his name. I wanted to tell him how Nick had drowned in an ornamental garden pond at my Mom and Dad's house and that, through his death, four other people hopefully would live. I would do that for Nick, because he deserved to be recognized.

For the next hour or so, Doug and I and our two angelic children (for they never once complained) waited shoulder to shoulder with the other organ donor families. It struck me as odd that Doug and I seemed to be the only two people having difficulty keeping our emotions in check. Doug succeeded where I failed, because I could not keep the tears from my eyes. There was no denying where we were and what we were there for. We were literally surrounded by "organ donation."

When at last it was our turn to enter the governor's

office, we were met by two men, one of whom was a funeral director from Nevada, Iowa, who had helped organize the event. They offered us their hands and, as they had graciously greeted the rest of the throng, asked us who we were honoring. I turned Nick's picture around and managed to squeak out the words, "Our son." It was clear from their expressions that they hadn't had many families pass through who had lost children.

The funeral director asked us when we had lost our son and again looked shocked when we told him it had only been two months. He asked what had caused Nick's death and when we told him, he put his hands to his mouth and took a step back. He quickly regained his composure and we were no longer faces in the crowd. "Where are you from?" We told him we were from St. Anthony, but that Nick's accident had taken place in Clinton. "I know about your family!" His church in Nevada had prayed for us. We didn't know one blessed soul from that church, and they didn't know us, but they had prayed for Nick.

Now my tears were with gratitude for this stranger, who no longer seemed like a stranger. He had cared about Nick and had prayed for his recovery. He continued to talk with us as we waited, paying special attention to Allison and Kate. He told us what we could expect when we stepped through "the door" into the governor's offices.

At last, it was our turn to go through the doorway. We were ushered through three rooms, and in each room there were two government officials. With each shake of the hand we told these individuals about Nick. We received the same reaction each time: shock mingled with empathy. The telling didn't get easier with repetition, and Doug and I basically left a trail of tears as we passed through the extravagant rooms.

Finally, and mercifully, we reached the last pair of hands to shake and I was able to tell Allie, "That one is the governor." She was excited to meet and shake the hand of a famous person. I thought, "This is for you, Nick," as I shook the governor's hand and told Nick's story one last time. I expected to hear a prepared response to our situation, so was surprised when the governor appeared to be speechless. He didn't know what to say and said as much. But his eyes spoke volumes. They were filled with compassion and gratitude for Nick having given the gift of life.

I left the room feeling a deep respect for the governor. He had held and looked at Nick's picture, and Doug and I both felt that he had truly listened to what we had said about our son. Finally, he had nothing to say, which actually said a lot more than had he issued forth a bunch of empty, prepared statements. We learned later that the governor's sister had received a heart transplant, so I think he had genuine respect and deep appreciation for the organ donation process.

After our ordeal was over, and it truly was an ordeal, we were given a red rose in honor of our loved one. We were then led out into the large expanse of the outer room. It seemed less crowded, and I was feeling a tremendous sense of relief and accomplishment. I was proud of us for staying and thought that Nick would be smiling down at us from heaven.

As I followed Doug towards the exit, I felt someone grab hold of my arm. It was Amney. Apparently, she had seen us at some point and had recognized us. Having just made it through the governor's office, talking with Amney no longer seemed like such a monumental task. I grabbed

Doug before he could get too far, and we had a very brief but nice conversation with Amney. She told us that she had been waiting for us to get through the line and had taken a picture of us shaking hands with the governor. We hadn't thought to bring a camera, so we were grateful to her for her thoughtfulness. We visited briefly and answered her questions on how we had been coping. She gave us all hugs and said she hoped to see us at organ donor events in the future.

We left the Iowa State Capitol that day feeling like we had accomplished something great. We laid the rose in front of our headstone at the cemetery and I put Nick's Certificate of Gratitude, complete with the Iowa State Seal, in the scrapbook that I had started for him. Nick had been honored by many influential people that day, and he would be honored by us, his family, every day.

Two days after our visit to the Capitol, we received our first letter from one of Nick's recipients. I had walked to the end of our gravel driveway hopeful that there would be a letter marked with the ODN return address, but knowing that once again I would be disappointed. But this day, I was anything but disappointed.

From the first moment that I saw the familiar return address, I told myself that the letter probably contained a letter or an update from the Organ Donor Network itself. They were very good about sending us letters of support and letters containing dates for special events, etc. When I pulled the envelope out from the pile of bills and junk mail, however, I could feel that there was another smaller and thicker envelope inside. My heart started to pound in my chest immediately, realizing what I was most certainly holding. I sprinted back up the drive wanting nothing more that to rip the letter open and read what I hoped would be a correspondence from one of Nick's recipients. Once in the house, however, I knew that I couldn't open the letter without Doug. I fought the irresistible urge to take just a peek and dialed Doug's work number praying that I wouldn't get his answering machine. I'm sure I must have let out a huge sigh of relief when I heard, "Hello, this is Doug," on the other end of the line. "Hi, it's me. I think we got a letter!" Struggling to hold the phone between my shoulder and my ear, I fumbled to open the letter. Inside the main envelope there was a letter from the ODN and another smaller, yellow envelope. There was no address on the yellow envelope. This was it. This was what we had been waiting for. I was shaking as I read, out loud, the letter from the ODN:

Dear Doug and Erin,

 Recently, I received correspondence for you from Nicholas's Liver/Small Bowel recipient. I have enclosed it in a sealed envelope so that you may open it when you are ready. If you wish to return a letter or a card to this recipient I will be happy to forward any correspondence.
 Please know you continue to be in our thoughts. If there is anything I can do for you please do not hesitate to call me.
 Wishing you peace and comfort,
 Julie
 Donor Family Coordinator

I laid the white piece of paper on the kitchen counter and picked up the yellow envelope. I thought, briefly, that I should get a letter opener out and open the envelope neatly, but then my anxiety got the better of me and I slipped my index finger under the corner and started to rip.

Inside was a sheet of white paper, It had been folded many times so that it would fit inside the too small envelope. I unfolded the letter slowly and deliberately, feeling that, whatever I was about to read, would change my life forever.

The first thing I noticed was that the letter had been typed using a computer and the author had chosen one of the slanted fonts. The next thing I noticed was the date printed in the upper right hand corner: October 29, 2001. The date told me that the letter had been written before the family had received my letter. It made me feel good that they had chosen to write of their own accord, and that they weren't just responding to a letter from us.

I took a deep breath and started to read the letter out loud to Doug. I'm not sure he was able to make out all of the words that I read to him as the pure emotion and magnitude of the letter sank into my heart and my soul. We learned of what this little girl's life had been like before her transplant. Due to the short bowel syndrome that she had, she had endured eighteen surgeries by the age of two, and much of her days were spent connected to machines. They described their daughter as smart, happy, and possessing a very strong will to live. The family sent their condolences for our loss and thanked us for making a decision that helped save their daughter's life. Nick's liver and bowel had given her a chance at a normal life free of machines.

My expectations for this first communication from one of Nick's recipients had been met one hundred-fold. To hear that Nick was recognized as a giver of life were words that I needed to hear. I think that letter, written by another mother who desperately loved her child, went a long way in helping me find the path that would help lead me in the direction of healing.

After reading and rereading the precious letter, I sat down at the computer and wrote a reply. I hated that it would be weeks before the family would receive my letter and then additional weeks before I would hear back from them. Procedures had to be followed, however, and I would do my best to be patient.

December 16, 2001

Dear Recipient and Family,

    We were so excited to receive your letter (Dec. 10). I couldn't wait for Doug to get home to read your letter, so I called him at work and read it to him over the phone.

    I can not tell you how pleased we are that, through our tragedy, your precious little girl has a chance at a better life. I can't think of anything more comforting than knowing that, although we were helpless to save Nicholas, we were not helpless when it came to the chance to try and save another life. We believe that Nick would be very proud of our decision, as he was a very loving and caring little boy in life.

    Nick was two years old when he had his accident. He drowned in a small, ornamental garden pond while we were visiting my parents. Doug, and then the rescue team, performed CPR on Nick and were able to resuscitate him, but the injuries to his brain from lack of oxygen were too severe. He was pronounced brain dead five days later. We know that we were given a gift when we were able to have him back for those five days. Not only could we tell him all of the things that we wanted to tell him, but we were also given the opportunity to give the gift of life through organ donation.

Nicholas was truly a wonderful little boy. He has two sisters, Allison (7 ½) and Kate (5), and he loved to play with them. Besides playing with his sisters, Nick loved to be outside swinging on the swing, riding on the tractor with his daddy, or digging in the dirt. He was always picking up rocks and putting them in his jeans pockets or in his bucket. He liked to play with his toy cars and play catch with balls, but he was also known to carry around his sisters' baby dolls (he loved babies). His favorite movies were A Bug's Life and Toy Story. He would watch them over and over. When he wasn't playing, Nick loved to be read to. He would snuggle up on my lap with his "Oppie" (burp rag or cloth diaper) and I would read to him book after book.

Nicholas was an absolute joy to our family, just as I know your daughter is a joy to your family. She sounds like a beautiful little girl and we are so honored to have had the opportunity to help her. She has become quite the celebrity around here, as we have told all of our friends and family about her. We will continue to pray for her that everything goes well.

Bless you all for your courage and strength. Know that, although we are not with you in person, we are with you in thought and spirit.

Your donor family,
Doug, Erin, Allison and Kate

I signed our names in my best penmanship, irritated that I was unable to add our last name. Then I folded the letter so that all of the edges lined up perfectly. I wanted very badly to send a picture of Nick with the letter, but didn't want to rush things and send the family more than they could handle. I could hardly wait to see the precious face of the child that was chosen to receive organs from Nicholas, and I hoped that the next letter we received would contain a photo.

As the days turned colder and the holiday season approached, it became necessary to start thinking about Christmas. I again felt as if I were just going through the motions, putting on a show of sorts, as Doug and I lugged the boxes of Christmas decorations out of the attic. For the first time in my life I felt no joy or anticipation as the boxes of ornaments and lights started to fill the upstairs bedroom.

The task of unpacking our years of accumulated decorations felt overwhelming to me, so I made a compromise to myself and only took out the decorations that were on the top of each box.

When I got to the box marked ornaments, I chuckled to myself as I remembered last Christmas and one very special Christmas ornament. Allison had been about six years old. I was in the kitchen when she came storming up the steps. She was obviously furious about something, and from the tone she was using, Kate was involved. I finally slowed her down enough to gather that Kate had eaten her favorite ornament. I dutifully went to investigate this horrendous injustice, and had to suppress my urge to laugh as I found a very guilty looking Kate standing in front of the Christmas tree downstairs. She was looking down at her hands as if she had never noticed them before. She glanced up at me and I almost lost my composure when I noticed the red, sticky goo around her pouting mouth.

At that moment Allie stomped over holding out the incriminating evidence, her kindergarten ornament, lovingly made out of round peppermint candies that had been melted together to form a circle. A five-year-old Allison smiled up at me from the photo that was affixed to the center, but, tragically, one side of the ornament had a big, mouth sized chunk out of it. Sticky strings of two-year- old candy trailed off to the side. Never mind that the once perfect circle of sweets was distorted from the heat of summer storage, the memories that it held for Allie were dear given her state of distress. Either that or this was just a really good opportunity to get her sister in trouble.

I did my best stern mother impression and looked at Kate, one eyebrow raised and lips pursed. "Kate?" Don't smile, don't smile, don't smile, I repeated in my mind. How many punishments had I ruined because I couldn't control my expressions? "Did you eat Allie's ornament?" Still engrossed in her hands, she silently shook her head "no." At that moment there was a commotion from under the Christmas tree. Baby Nick, who had witnessed the candy consumption, was bound and determined that there was still food in that tree and he was going to have some. As I looked at my children; Allie still glaring at Kate and waiting for me to deliver justice, Kate who was denying that she had partaken of her sister's Christmas ornament, and Nick, who had "crawled" under the tree and was reaching his arms up pleading with someone to share the goods with him. Although I had done very well up until that point, I couldn't help laughing at the absurdity of the whole scenario.

I told the kids to stay where they were and I ran upstairs to get the camera. I had learned that these moments almost always ended up being funny, and someday I would share these beautiful memories with my children. Plus, going to get the camera usually gave me time to cool off if I really was mad. When I felt like spanking someone's bottom, the walk to get the camera gave me the time that I needed so that when I got back, all I felt like doing was taking a picture of it.

And so that is what I did. I stood Kate in front of the Christmas tree and had her hold the ornament up in front of her like a prison ID. As I took her picture I wondered if I should have called poison control. The two-year-old candy didn't worry me so much as what may have been on it as a preservative.

My smile slipped away and my memory of that day went back into storage as I closed the ornament box and moved on to the box marked "stockings." Without opening the box, I could see Nick's red stocking neatly folded, his name written in silver glitter on the white felt at the top. It had been packed away last year with a little bit of sadness for another Christmas gone by, but also with a great deal of satisfaction for another holiday season well done.

There was no hesitation when making the decision to hang Nick's stocking once again in its rightful place next to Allison's and Kate's stockings. There was, however, a great deal of sadness in the act of hanging it. I wanted so badly for Nicholas to be with us for Christmas and I felt a desperate need to include him in everything that we did, perhaps because of my deep belief that he was still with us in spirit and was aware of all we did to keep him involved. I refused to let him go in any other way except in body. The rest was mine for keeps.

Once the decorations were in place, my next task was to begin Christmas shopping. In addition to strolling up and down the girl aisles, I automatically went down the aisles whose shelves were stacked with cars and action figures. At two years old, Nick hadn't really asked for specific toys, but I knew him well enough to know which toys would light up his eyes and make him reach out his hand. In my mind, I bought those toys, wrapped them, and watched Nick's joy as he opened them on Christmas morning. Sitting amid the torn gift wrap, his chubby fingers would try to open the boxes, but when he failed to get past the tape and ribbons, he'd bring the boxes to Daddy and watch expectantly as the toys were set free.

It hurt tremendously not buying gifts for Nick. My rational mind knew that Nick didn't want for anything, but I couldn't shake the feeling that I was neglecting or even disappointing Nick in some way. So it was with great relief that the perfect solution presented itself a few days later.

Allison brought home from school a flyer for Toys for Tots. We had given toys to Toys for Tots in the past and it occurred to me that this year we could donate toys that we would have bought for Nick. It was a wonderful feeling to take the girls shopping and tell them to pick out a toy for Nick. Allison and Kate seemed very pleased with the idea, and put a lot of thought into their choices. They passed up the toys for big boys and limited their selections to the "three and under" items. Nicholas ended up with a Tonka truck pulling a space shuttle and a talking Howie the Hacksaw. When we got home, the girls sat on the couch and held their gifts for Nick. I took their picture with the intention of putting the photo in Nick's scrapbook, and then put the toys back in the bag so that Allie could take them to school in the morning.

I felt satisfied with our purchases for Nick, so I was unprepared for the dilemma that I ran into when I was finishing up my shopping for the girls. It was a Saturday morning and Doug stayed home with Allie and Kate so that I could get the last of my secret shopping done. I had gone to the outlet mall in Story City and was cruising the aisles of the toy store when I saw the Woody doll. From the moment I saw the doll I knew that Nick would have loved it. Toy Story was one of Nick's favorite movies, but instead of saying he wanted to watch Toy Story, he would say that he wanted to watch Woody.

Our budget didn't allow for over spending, so I walked around the store for what seemed an eternity, pretending to be looking at toys, when in actuality, I was deciding whether or not I should buy the Woody doll for

Nick. I knew there were about fifty other places that eleven dollars would be needed, but I couldn't get over the image of Nick's eyes lighting up as he saw that toy. Had he been living, I would have bought the doll without a second's hesitation. With that realization, I went back and picked the Woody off of the shelf.

With a strange sense of determination, I carried the toy to the counter, half expecting someone to question me as to why I was buying the toy. I was already thinking of how I was going to justify my purchase to Doug. But then a feeling of warmth came over me as I realized that he would understand and there wouldn't be a need to justify my purchase. When I got home, we decided that the Woody doll would be just right sticking out of Nick's stocking on Christmas morning.

In the evenings when the girls went to bed, Doug and I did our best communicating. It was during one of these evening discussions, snuggling side by side under a blanket on the couch, that we decided to get a puppy in time for Christmas. We had been talking about getting a puppy for over a year, ever since we had lost our dog Quantum to bone cancer. We had previously decided that the puppy would be Nick's dog because the girls each had a cat and a rabbit to call their own. We had been thinking that the summer of Nick's third birthday would be an appropriate time to get the dog, but circumstances being as they were, we decided that this Christmas would be the perfect time to introduce a little bundle of joy (and diversion) into the family. Doug got busy with the classifieds. Many phone calls and a visit later, he had a black lab puppy chosen (with impeccable hunting genes). Born on Halloween, our little round ball of fur and teeth was ready for pick up the week before Christmas. Doug came up with a brilliant story for the puppy's early arrival under the tree. It seemed that on Christmas night, Santa's sleigh was so full of gifts that there wasn't room for puppies, so Santa delivered "live" gifts early.

So Takoda, whose whole AKC name is Nick's Buddy Takoda, or as I liked to call her, @#$%^, made a wonderful entrance into our lives in a brightly wrapped Christmas package. Later I would tell Doug that had the big red bow been around her muzzle instead of around her neck, we wouldn't have matching holes in the recliner and the carpet, not to mention all of the new clothes we got for Christmas that year! We wanted a diversion, and by golly, we got one!

The girls were beside themselves with joy and I must admit that I watched the dog for signs of "familiarity." I had heard that the spirits of loved ones could make their presence known through family pets. It didn't take me long to conclude that if any spirit were working through our puppy, it wasn't the heavenly kind.

December continued on in a blur of activity. I sent out Christmas cards, but unable to put any thought into them, I just signed our names. I threw away many cards until I painfully got used to not signing Nick's name. Signing Nick's name felt like telling a lie, but leaving his name off of our family's cards felt like a betrayal. So, I compromised and, somewhere on everyone's card, I drew a very simple little angel. I knew I would appear pathetic to some people, but better pathetic than neglectful.

Christmas morning arrived with a mixture of emotion, joy, and gratitude that Allison and Kate had Christmas cheer in abundance, waking Doug and I up at the crack of dawn because Santa had left a sleigh load of gifts under our tree. But the day also arrived with a great deal of sorrow. Woody dangled out of the top of Nick's stocking, never to feel the chubby little hands of his owner. And Takoda jumped and barked at the baby gate that had been strategically placed to keep our Christmas from being chewed to bits, never to run and chase the little feet of her intended boy.

I oohed and aahed as the girls opened their gifts, smiling at them with the false smile that I hoped would camouflage the deep loneliness and despair that I was feeling. In the center of the tree was a picture of Nick in a Christmas tree frame. As I looked at his smiling face, I told myself that Nick wasn't really missing Christmas. He was with us in his own way, and I believed that he was part of a much greater celebration in heaven. Imagine spending Christmas with Jesus! I did my best to let that thought bring me comfort, and I think to some extent it did.

When the Christmas season finally drew to a close, a trip to Northwood and a trip to Clinton later, I sat down one night to write in Nick's baby book. As I did with all of the kids' books, I wrote as if I were talking to that child. So I wrote to Nick and I told him how much we had missed him. I told him how we had visited the cemetery on the way home from the Christmas Eve service, and how we had stuck a Santa decoration in the ground next to the headstone. I told him how we had left milk and cookies out for Santa and carrots for the reindeer and how we had been to visit all of our family. Then I told him about the gifts that he had received; a puppy, two ornaments, a zebra book that Kate had picked out on our last visit to the book store, a Woody doll, and, of course, the Tonka truck and talking tools. I told him that because of him, some little boys somewhere were having a very nice Christmas.

As I finished writing and was closing Nick's book, I thought to myself, that somewhere there were four families who would be celebrating a very special, very blessed holiday season. For as much pain as our family felt, somewhere there were four families whose pain had been eased by the life giving gift of our little boy. The thought of what those families must be experiencing, having their loved ones with them for another holiday, brought a wonderful peace and solace to my soul. I closed my eyes, took a deep breath and whispered to Nick's picture on our Christmas tree, "Merry Christmas."

Throughout the holiday season and into the new year, the feeling of emptiness and loss that I had been feeling intensified. I felt as if I were struggling with who I was and who I wanted to be. The "who I was" part of me had been changed by Nick's death. I had been the mother of two school aged daughters and one two- year- old son. I saw to it that the girls got to school at the appropriate times and, while I was waiting for them to come home, I made cookies and did dishes with a little boy wrapped around my legs. At bedtime I tucked three children into bed, one of them repeatedly. I bought Barbie underwear for two little girls, and did my best to get one little boy to be interested in sitting on the potty chair (unsuccessfully).

At the grocery store I had the youngest one in the front of the cart and the middle one in the basket, while the big one complained that she had to walk. We had routines and schedules and traditions. It was comfortable and it was good. But after Nick died, everything changed and everything felt wrong. I felt as though I had not only lost Nick, but my job as well. My identity as a mother had changed, and I wasn't ready for it to change. I wasn't ready to be finished tending to a baby.

As I lay in bed at night, alone with my thoughts, I began to seriously consider what it might mean for me, and for all of us, to have another baby in our family. I thought of how it would feel to have a tiny baby snuggling up under my chin. I thought of Allie and Kate being big sisters again, and I thought of how I would love to have new life brought into our family to wipe out the painful image of death taking it away. But as I considered what a baby could mean for us, I was terrified of what my motives genuinely were. My greatest fear was that, somewhere in the back of my mind, I was trying to replace Nick or to bring him back. I truly didn't feel that was my purpose, but did I really know my grieving mind well enough to make that decision on my own?

I don't recall the circumstances under which I first broached the baby subject to Doug, but I do remember his initial response. "No." I expected him to say as much, especially given the fact that he had endured a vasectomy when I was six months pregnant with Nick! I had rehearsed quite a list of reasons for having another baby, and apparently I was pretty convincing, because he did agree to consider the thought.

I expected to feel lightened somehow with the hope of

having another child, but in actuality, I ended up feeling weighed down with responsibility. I worried that I was trying to replace Nick and I worried that other people would think I was trying to replace Nick. I worried about what reversing the vasectomy would cost, and I worried about Doug undergoing the procedure only to have it fail. And I worried that something could go wrong with another pregnancy. I agonized over my decision, trying to weigh all of the pros and cons. I prayed to God asking for guidance and I talked to Nick, hoping for some sign from him as to what I should do. It mattered a great deal to me that he knew we would never replace him and I begged him for some sign to let me know he would welcome a new member into our family.

As I write this I think how silly I was to entertain such thoughts. I know what God and heaven mean for Nick, and I know Nick does not judge my actions. But as I looked to make such an enormous change in our family, I couldn't help but include him in the equation.

It was with a grateful heart that I received my answer from Nick one day in February. I was talking with the insurance company on the phone. The representative I had spoken with was familiar with our situation. We had talked many times throughout the past few months. I explained to her my desire to have another child, but that Doug would need to undergo a vasectomy reversal for that to be a possibility. I guess I had hoped to hear her say that, because of our circumstances, our insurance would cover some, if not all, of the procedure. But, those weren't the words that she was able to tell me. Although the vasectomy itself was virtually free, a reversal would not be covered. I was very disappointed by what I had learned and, although she couldn't tell me what the procedure would cost, I knew that it would be more than Doug and I could afford.

I felt almost as if I had already bonded with the baby that I wanted to carry and now I was saying good-bye before I could ever see its face. I hung up the phone and looked through tear-filled eyes out the window. A movement caught my eye and I watched, unbelieving, as an American Bald Eagle flew towards my window and looked me in the eye. I saw the clear blue eyes, every feather, and every detail as the majestic bird barely cleared the roof of the house.

I'm not sure how long I stood, dumbstruck, standing next to that window. I processed what I had seen, and it suddenly became very clear to me that I had been given the approval that I had sought. I now knew with certainty that I had been given a blessing, from either God or Nick, to pursue the change in our family that I needed. I felt like, whatever the obstacles, we could overcome them.

I didn't see the eagle after that morning, but as I told Doug what I had witnessed, we both agreed that it had definitely been sent by a heavenly hand. Living where we do, in the middle of farm fields, we had never before, nor have we since, seen eagles near our house.

I felt renewed with a purpose after that day. I made several calls; to the doctor who had delivered Nick, to the social worker at the hospital in Iowa City, to the Organ Donor Network, and to Amy, Nick's nurse. I asked them all the same questions: Do you think I am ready to make such an important decision so soon after the loss of our son? And, do you think I am making this decision for the right reasons? Amazingly they all encouraged us to have another child and gave us their blessings; all but one that is. The doctor (the one with the red high tops) who had delivered Nick didn't discourage us from having another baby, but he did make it very clear that vasectomy reversals only had a success rate of about 40%. He also told me that we could expect to pay anywhere from $4,000-$7,000 depending on who performed the procedure. The thought of spending that much money for Doug to undergo a painful procedure that might not even result in a pregnancy was a definite concern.

I was also concerned that our family headstone at the cemetery did not have room for the addition of any other children's names. On the back side of the stone would be carved the names of our children; Allison, Kate and Nick. Normally, the names of children would be surrounded by a box on the back side of their parents' headstone. In our case, however, since Doug and I were still young and of childbearing age, the box would be left off in case we had more children. When the "blueprints" arrived at our house for us to look over, neither Doug nor I gave any thought to the fact that there was a box around our children's names on the plan. It was difficult for us to check spellings and dates let alone look for other possible errors. So when we called the monument company we told them that everything was okay. It wasn't until Dec. 12, when the stone arrived at the cemetery, that we realized that the box was there. Even then it was of little consequence as it hadn't occurred to us then that we may choose to have more children.

Now, two months later, as we contemplated having another child, that simple box bothered me a great deal.

I wasn't comfortable with the thought of having another child and not being able to include his/her name with our other children's names. I called the company and explained my dilemma to the representative who answered. She informed me that there wasn't anything that could be done, because once the stone was cut, the process was irreversible. As I hung up the phone I felt like maybe we weren't supposed to have another baby. Discouraged but not defeated, I decided that there had to be a solution, and by the next day, I thought I might have come up with one.

Having spent a lot of time at the cemetery, I remembered seeing bronze plaques on some stones. A bronze plaque wouldn't be the perfect solution, but it would cover the existing names. I called the monument company back and this time reached the consultant who had worked with us the day we had ordered our stone. He remembered our family and, as I explained our dilemma, he said he remembered saying that they would not put the box around the children's names. I asked him if we could put a bronze plaque over the names on the back of the stone. His reply was that the box shouldn't have been on the stone, and if we had another child, the company would replace the whole monument for us... at no charge. He said he would mail us a letter, valid for ten years, stating that, should we have more children, his monument company would replace our headstone with a new one.

I was overwhelmed by his generosity and tried to tell him that we felt responsible for not having made the correction when the plans had come to us for our approval. Despite my reasoning, he insisted on making the correction with a new stone rather than covering the mistake with a plaque. I thanked him again and hung up the phone, anxious to tell Doug once again that God was on our side and we had been blessed yet again.

Doug and I had many heart to heart discussions after that day, weighing the pros and cons, trying our best to look into the future and see the possible outcomes of our decision to have another child. In the end, we made the decision to go ahead with the surgery and prayed that all would go well. Doug called the same doctor who had performed his vasectomy and scheduled an appointment for the first week in April. I felt excited and hopeful for the first time since Nick's accident, confident that we had made the right choice for our family.

Chapter 6

In-between discussions about increasing our family, Doug and I had another decision that we were trying to make. The money that had been raised for us by the benefit in Zearing was still in a memorial account at the bank. We had always known that we wanted to use the money for a memorial to Nick, but we hadn't as yet decided what we wanted to do. We had considered giving the money to the Pediatric Intensive Care Unit at the hospital in Iowa City. We had also thought about giving the money to the Children's Miracle Network who had been very supportive of us when Nick had been in the hospital. But we also wanted to be able to "see" a memorial to Nick, something that was tangible, and that in life he would have liked.

That was when we got the idea for the playground. We thought of the picnic we had in Story City when Eric, Vickie and David had come to visit and we thought of how much fun the kids had on the playground equipment there. It was the same equipment that Nick had been playing on when the picture had been taken of him that I wore on my necklace.

Once we started thinking along the lines of the playground, the idea became the perfect solution for our needs. The Zearing Park didn't have a lot for children Nick's age to play on, and since the people of Zearing were the reason that we had a memorial account the size that we did, it was a way that we could give back to the community that was so good to us.

We revisited the park in Story City to see if we could find the name of the company that had made the playground that we liked. The label on the piece of equipment said that it was made by the Miracle Recreation Equipment Company. When we got home we contacted the company, told them what we had in mind and arranged for a meeting with a representative.

In late January we met our contact at the park in Zearing. He looked over the park and we agreed on a good location for the playground equipment. There was an open area between trees and not far from the older children's climber. The site could also be seen from the nursing home across the road, offering a colorful view of the kids at play.

After we had decided on a good site for the playground, we resumed the meeting at our house. We gave the sales representative a general idea of what we had in mind and how much money we had to spend. We wanted something geared for the younger kids, with as many choices of activities as possible. He had a catalogue and showed us, one piece at a time, exactly what we had in mind. By the end of the hour, he had designed the perfect piece of playground equipment for our memorial to Nick; a primary colored climber for ages 2-12. It would have a mogul slide, tot rock climber, crawl tube, side by side slides, wall with a steering wheel, honeycomb climber, vertical ladder, and three decks. We ended up spending slightly more than what we had planned on, but had been able to include much more than we had thought possible.

A few days later, we received a top view and colored rendering of the structure we had designed. The next step was to present our proposed playground equipment to the Zearing Park Board. Doug handled the meeting himself, showing the computer generated plans and explaining the location we had in mind. He also explained that we would need help with ground preparation and volunteers to help put the equipment together. The park board approved our proposal and a tentative date was set for April 18th to begin construction.

With all of the details approved and finalized my stress level subsided and I felt a sense of peace and accomplishment. I knew without a doubt that Nick would be pleased that we had chosen a fitting memorial for him. I was sad that he would never have the chance to play on the equipment, but I felt good that his friends, sisters, and strangers as well, would enjoy it on his behalf.

As events in our lives seemed to be taking a positive turn, I was thrilled the afternoon of Jan. 26, 2002 to go out to the mailbox and find a letter from the ODN. It was thick which I had come to learn meant that there was a second letter inside. I rushed back to the house and, without taking my coat off, opened up the letter to see who it was from. The letter was a response to the one I had sent to Nick's liver and bowel recipient and her family a month previously. I dialed Doug's work number and, when he picked up, began reading the letter out loud.

The letter started out saying how happy they were to receive correspondence from us so soon. The little girl's mother wrote of similarities between things that I had written Nick had liked and things that her daughter had just recently come to like since her transplant; movies, such as Toy Story, playing in the dirt and just loving people in general.

The letter continued to say how sorry they were to hear how Nick had passed away, but that we should be very proud that we had let him live on in a different form. She then wrote that our letter could not have come at a better time. They had just arrived home to pack because their daughter had been very sick and was going to have to go back in the hospital. The doctors were afraid that she might be rejecting her organs. When they pulled into the driveway of their home, the mother said she told her husband that there was a letter from their donor family. He checked and, sure enough, our letter was there. After reading the letter, she cried and knew that everything would be alright.

I had enclosed a picture of Nick, so it was the first time that they had seen him. She said she felt a mixture of happiness and sadness receiving it. Happiness because looking at Nick's face, she knew that everything was going to be alright, and sadness because she knew that our baby was gone.

The next paragraph that I read aloud to Doug has become etched forever in my memory. When I need to be reminded of God's divine love and the promise of heaven, I reread her words in my mind.

Their two-year-old daughter had been so sick that she did not want to get out of bed. For two days it had been a struggle for her to stay awake, let alone play. When her mother showed her Nick's picture, she smiled, got up out of bed and started playing. By the next day she was up and smiling as if she had never been sick. Doctors still checked the child for rejection and when they found nothing, they checked her for viruses. Again, they found nothing. In fact, they were at a loss to explain what had caused her to be so sick. Her parents couldn't explain her illness and neither could we, but I think we both agreed on what had made her better.

Not knowing one another's spiritual preferences, we had not brought up the subject of religion before, but under the circumstances, we both felt that their daughter had a very special little angel watching over her. A little angel who her parents credited with not only making their daughter better, but who also made their daughter laugh when there was no one else is around.

Encouraged by this little one's miraculous recovery, I wrote a letter to Nick's heart recipient. The baby girl, three months old when she had received her heart transplant, would now be nine months old. I was desperate to have contact with her family, needing to hear that she was healthy, but also needing to know if they had "felt" Nick's presence around their baby.

It dawns on me now as I'm writing, that I viewed the stories I had heard as communication or verification that Nick still existed in a very heavenly form. I wholeheartedly believed that life continued after death, but a little proof never hurt and I felt reassured in my beliefs.

Knowing that some recipient families felt guilt that their loved ones had benefited from the death of another, I wrote in my letter that we continued to be comforted by our decision to donate Nick's organs. We had been given the opportunity to take a horrible tragedy and make something good come of it. I wrote that when they were ready, I wanted to hear all about their baby, her health, and their family, and in turn, I would like to tell them about Nick. I kept my letter short, not wanting to overwhelm the family, but I needed them to understand that, in our case, hearing from them would be a tremendous comfort.

Comfort came to us one week later, not in the form of a letter from Nick's heart recipient, but in the form of a photo from his liver and bowel recipient. The family's previous letter had said that a photo was enclosed and we had been very disappointed to find that there was no photo in the envelope. The ODN had sent a note saying that when they had received the correspondence, there hadn't been a photo either.

But this time when we received the letter from the ODN, there were two envelopes inside. One envelope contained a letter from the little girl's family and the other contained a photo. Like a child who can't wait to open a gift until after the birthday card is read, I immediately opened the photo first. It is difficult to describe the feeling that I felt looking into the eyes of the little miracle who had received the gift of life from our son.

She was small and beautiful. Her dark hair was tied up in two little pony tails, but it was her eyes and expression that spoke volumes to me. Her dark brown eyes were looking off to the side where I am sure her mom and dad were standing, trying their best to get her to smile for the photographer. She wasn't smiling and looked like she wanted to cry. Her cheeks were puffy due to the medications that she had to take, and in her arms she clutched a fuzzy, brown teddy bear. She looked very much like a little girl who had been through a lot of pain and suffering in her short life and my heart went out to her.

As I continued to look at the precious little face, the thought occurred to me that I was being introduced to someone who was already dear to our son. I relate the feeling to how I think it would be if Nick were in college and he called us on the phone saying he had just met someone he really cared for and he couldn't wait for us to meet her. I could almost picture the two of them together, although strictly in a spiritual sense.

After what must have been several minutes, I laid down the photo and picked up the letter. It was a letter updating us on the child's medical condition. Her mother wrote how her ostomy bag had been removed two months ahead of schedule because she was doing so well. She wrote that the picture she had sent had been taken four months after the transplant. She had planned to send us a photo taken before the transplant, so we could see how healthy her daughter looked by comparison, but she wasn't at home to find one at the time she had mailed the letter to us.

I felt slightly disappointed not to have the other photos. One picture only increased my desire for more. After seeing the little girl's face I felt that I knew her better, and I craved to know even more. I wanted to see her family, her home, her bedroom, how she looked in the morning when she has just woken up. I knew that given the opportunity, I would meet with their family, hug them and kiss them despite the fact that they were really just strangers to us. I pictured myself crying and running into their arms like in a beach scene from an old movie. The connection I felt was incredible. I felt love for someone that I didn't even know, and all because of a terrible tragedy that took our son from us and saved their daughter.

As spring approached and the weather turned mild, our thoughts turned towards the final preparations for Nick's memorial playground. I received a call one morning from a newspaper reporter from the "Nevada Journal." She had been told about our project and wanted to know if she could interview Doug and me for an article in her paper. I told her that I would be happy to do an interview, but I felt awkward that it would be about our family donating a playground to the park. I didn't want to come across as though we were seeking recognition for our "generous donation" to the city of Zearing. I asked the reporter if, instead of focusing on the playground, if we could focus on Nick, his life, and his gift. I was relieved when she agreed to my proposition.

Doug's work schedule didn't allow him to go to the interview with me, so I went to do it by myself. I took Nick's scrapbook with me, not knowing what I would be asked, and how many details I might need to recall. The reporter, Marlys, and I were about the same age, and I could see that she was also a mother from the pictures sitting on the shelf behind her desk.

As we started the interview, Marlys simply asked me to tell her about Nick. At first I was a little nervous, and I wasn't sure where to begin. I decided to just trust my instincts (and God), and the first sentence out of my mouth, and the first sentence to appear in the article was, "He was wonderful."

The words just flowed out of my mouth after that and

as I talked, Marlys typed. Both of us cried. As a mother of young children (triplets!), I think she could empathize with how it might feel to lose a child herself. After I had finished telling Marlys about Nick, his accident, and his organ donation, the information she took down about the playground seemed inconsequential.

I left the newspaper office feeling good about the article, and I felt that I had done something important for Nick and organ donor awareness. Like the saying goes, "If you can just help one person then it was all worthwhile." If I could persuade one person to look at their child with newfound respect, and if I could persuade one person to look at organ donation in a positive light, then I was glad to have been a part of the enlightening.

Several days after giving the newspaper interview, Marlys e-mailed us a copy of the article that she had written. I was shocked at the length of what she had written and was equally stunned at the content. By the time I had finished reading the article, much of which was word for word what I had said, I felt as though I was seeing our story through the eyes of someone else.

Nick's story appeared in the newspaper, March 14, 2002. On the front page was a 5x7 color photo of Nicholas. The headline read, "Others live thanks to Zearing boy." Any uneasiness I had over agreeing to the article faded as I was filled with feelings of pride. Underneath Nick's picture was the statement, "Organs from 2-year-old Nicholas Hulshizer have been transplanted in four people whose ages varied from 3 months to 64 years." It became very clear to me that the article really had very little to do with me and had everything to do with Nick.

The article was continued from the bottom half of the

front page to the entire page of A3. Marlys had written about Nick, our trip to Clinton, his accident, organ donation, and how we were coping as a family. Off to the side, as an article unto itself, was a segment on the park equipment. It was a good article and I thanked God once again for his guidance.

April was an exciting month as Doug had survived his "surgery," and the day had finally come to construct the playground equipment at the Zearing park. Despite a few sprinkles and cloud cover, we had a wonderful group of supporters and volunteers to help with our efforts. A representative from the Miracle Recreation Equipment Company came to coordinate the construction, and we were blessed with the many capable hands of friends and community members to actually carry out the work.

Throughout the day, food and refreshments were served by women of the community, and by 8:00 that evening, the structure was complete. Allison and Kate begged to be allowed on the brightly colored, brand new equipment, but had to be told they would have to wait until the concrete had dried for the footings. Caution tape was tied around the perimeter of the playground and Doug and I thought about camping in the park to prevent other anxious children from climbing on the structure before it was set.

We ended up going home, mostly due to exhaustion, and by the next day everything was as it should be and Nick's memorial playground was finished. Finished that is except for the few final touches like the bronze plaque that we had ordered. It would read, "In loving memory of Nicholas Drew Hulshizer by his friends and family. 1999-2001." A couple of weeks later, the Zearing Park Board brought in pea gravel and purchased several new benches for the park. For the town of Zearing, the play structure was a way for our family to say, "Thank you for your support," and for our son, Nick, it was our way of saying, "We will never forget."

By the end of May school had ended and I was excited to have the girls back home with me. But with summer came the time of year that I had been dreading. We had almost come full circle in the year following Nick's death. We had hit all of the holidays and birthdays except for one.

I was emotional and teary for most of the month of June. I thought of June as Nick's month. As his birthday approached I tried to think of how I wanted to celebrate his special day. I wanted Nick's birthday to be a day of remembrance, but I also wanted it to be a celebration. I decided that we would celebrate his birthday as we always celebrated birthdays; cake, candles, ice cream, balloons, presents, and the happy birthday banner.

June 17 started out bright and sunny, but it was hard for me to see the light for the loneliness in my heart. I allowed myself to remember, trying to recapture every smell, touch and sound that I associated with Nick. I started out upstairs, looking through the drawers of Nick's dresser. With each drawer that I opened I gently ran my hand along the top layer of clothing. Nick's burpie and pajamas were lying haphazardly in the top drawer. He had used them before we had left for Clinton and I hadn't laundered them, but instead had put them away as they had been left. I picked his pajama top up and smelled it, giving a sigh that I thought they might still have smelled like him after all of these months.

With each shirt, pair of jeans, hat and jacket that I touched, I conjured up loving memories of Nick laughing and playing. In the bottom drawer were his shoes, blankets and Halloween costume. Again I was flooded with memories. I picked up Nick's little red, white and blue Nikes. I looked inside them and noticed how they were worn from his hours of playing in them. They were his first real pair of shoes. On the soles there was still dirt stuck in the tread. I could see Nick digging outside in the dirt where the ground had been dug up for the new septic system.

When I had gone through the last of Nick's things, I composed myself, and went back downstairs. Allison and Kate knew what day it was and had been unusually quiet. They could see that I had been crying and I simply told them, "I'm just sad about Nick." They both nodded, as if they understood. I tried to lighten the mood and asked them if they would like to have a picnic with Nick for his birthday. They thought that was a swell idea and we went to the kitchen to prepare a lunch.

We ate our lunches on a blanket next to Nick's headstone. We talked and reminisced about Nick, giggling at some of the funny things he had done and said. When we were finished, we packed up our picnic and drove over to the outlet mall in Story City to pick out plates and napkins for Nick's birthday party. Nick loved balls so we chose to give him a sports birthday with basketballs, footballs, and baseballs on the plates and napkins. The girls each picked out a balloon to tie on a shepherd's hook by his stone at the cemetery and I picked out some plain helium balloons to take home and tie onto the birthday boy's chair.

When we got home we made Nick a chocolate cake with white frosting. The girls put on sprinkles and we wrote with blue frosting, "Happy 3rd Birthday, Nick." We waited for Doug to get home, and after we had eaten supper, we celebrated Nick's birthday. We sang "Happy Birthday" and the girls blew out the candles. I passed out unbirthday presents, which we had always done, and the girls opened them with their usual enthusiasm.

After cake and presents, we each took one of the balloons from the back of Nick's chair and we each wrote a message to him. My balloon said "Happy birthday, Buddy. I love you and miss you. Love, Mommy." Allie and Kate drew pictures and Doug wrote something on his balloon, although I didn't see what it said. We took the balloons out in the backyard and at the same moment, let them go. We watched the balloons float higher and higher until they were nothing but tiny specks in the sky. Kate wanted to know if they would float all the way up to heaven. I told her that I was sure they would.

For Doug and I, Nick's birthday party had been a painful experience. As hard as it was, however, I don't think it was an occasion that I could have let pass unnoticed or uncelebrated. I think the party was good for Allison and Kate. It gave them a happy occasion in which to think about and remember their brother. We had made Nick's birthday a fun, but memorable experience and I felt that Nick would approve.

As the days grew warmer, the girls started to beg me to take them swimming. Eventually, I found the courage to take the girls to the pool. Once there, however, I found it harder than normal to keep track of their wet little heads amidst the sea of other wet little heads. I watched the girls like a hawk, but I was also drawn to the "little ones" who were splashing about in their swim diapers. It was as I was watching that area of the pool that I saw a little boy, about two years old, come running toward the edge of the pool.

I watched, unbelieving, as he did the very thing that I feared. His little feet tried to stop as he reached the edge of the pool, but the rest of him kept going. In the blink of an eye he was face-down in the pool and was struggling to get his feet under him. I ran to the edge of the pool and was about to go in when I saw a child next to the boy looking at him. I think I screamed several times at the child, "Get him!" As if he were stuck in molasses, the child finally grabbed hold of the toddler and pulled his head out of the water.

The little boy didn't cry, but looked shocked as he tried to breathe. As the child coughed up water and attempted to fill his lungs with air, I saw the woman I assumed to be his mother, casually walk over to the edge of the pool. Apparently, she hadn't witnessed what had happened, but had gathered that the baby had either jumped or fallen into the pool. I was shaking uncontrollably by then and was feeling very angry at her nonchalance about the whole episode. She saw me standing at the edge of the pool and just shook her head like the little guy was always in trouble, a nuisance to deal with.

I went back to my post at the table, and after being assured that Allie and Kate were still okay, I began sobbing uncontrollably. Another mother at a table nearby saw me, and so she wouldn't think I was some kind of a nut, I explained that our two-year-old son had recently drowned. She expressed her sincere condolences, but didn't know what else to say, which was okay, since neither did I.

The other mother, however, continued to bother me as she sat in the shallow end of the pool sunbathing with her friend. The two women visited and seemed oblivious to their young children playing in the water. Normally, the old me would have said a quick prayer for the little ones and I would have gone on about my business. But this me was set to "do battle" in an effort to force them to see how precious and fragile their children were.

I took a deep breath and walked over to the two friends. I tried to minimize the shaking in my voice as I asked the mother if her son was alright. I think she recognized me as the quivering mass who had stood at the edge of the pool as she had plucked her little boy out of the water. She looked around her to locate the child and said, "Oh, yeah, he's okay." I responded to her by saying that I was sorry if I had overreacted, it was just that our two-year-old son had recently drowned. I again got the speechless reaction followed by how sorry she was for our loss. I told her, "Yes, it's very hard."

I had planted the thought that I wanted to plant and went back to my seat at the table. Moments later I saw that mother sitting on a bench at the side of the pool. She had her son, wrapped in a towel, sitting on her lap, and was whispering something in his ear.

The hot and muggy days of August arrived. One evening as Doug and I were outside working on Takoda's kennel, Allison came up to me and, out of the blue said, "Mom, do you think God can send Nick back to us in another baby?" I was stunned and speechless at what had come out of her 8-year-old mouth. Doug and I had decided not to tell the girls that we were hoping to have another baby, because we weren't sure that we could. I couldn't imagine what had triggered such a profound thought in the mind of our oldest daughter.

I don't recall exactly what my response was to Allison's question. I think I said something like, "If God wants us to have another baby, then we will, but the baby wouldn't be Nick." Later that night as I lay in bed I thought about what Allie had said. I wanted Nick back in our lives desperately, and I thought about what I had heard a psychic say on television about souls being reborn into the same family. I admit to liking the idea of having a new baby boy who would be very like the little boy we had lost. But then I thought about Nick in heaven, in the place that we all hope to be. I thought about making him leave that perfect place to come back to a place where there was pain and suffering, violence, and fear. We could love him and help him to find happiness, but it would always be mixed in with what is ugly in this existence. I would never want that for Nick and would rather meet him in heaven than have him come back to us here.

As school time neared, I began to think about what it was that I needed to do for myself. The girls would be gone during the days and I didn't like the idea of being alone all day every day with my thoughts. I began searching the internet for local job postings and was excited to find two openings with the Head Start Program. I decided to apply for both, one was full time and the other one was covering a three month maternity leave. I was fortunate enough to be called in for an interview for the three month maternity leave, and then even more fortunate when I had the position offered to me.

I looked forward to being a part of society again and began going to the Head Start training sessions. Coincidentally, I already knew the teacher I would be filling in for. Our two oldest children attended the same school and Pam's son, Bryce, was the same age as Nick. The boys had actually gone to story hour together. In any event, it felt good to be back in the work force and it felt even better to be a part of a program where I could make a difference in the lives of some very deserving kids. Pam went to all of the trainings with me and I was able to learn a lot about what was expected of me in the weeks before she took her leave.

One of the final courses required was the First Aid/CPR class. I was uncomfortable about taking the CPR portion of the class and had made myself almost sick worrying about it. On the ride to the college the morning of the class, I talked to Pam about my misgivings. She had taught the class herself and assured me that it would be relatively quick and that if I needed to leave the room at any point that I would be able to do that.

As we walked into the classroom, I remember talking to God, asking him to give me the strength to make it through the class without making a spectacle of myself. I reminded myself that it was routine for all teachers to be CPR certified. I was taking the class so that I could help children should the need arise. But I could not help but feel Nick's cold, tiny lips under mine as I tried to blow my breath into his lungs. I felt the water spurting from his nose as it hit my face, and I heard the water gurgling in his chest. I had been CPR certified several times and wasn't able to help save my own son.

By the time the first half of the class was over, I was so preoccupied with my thoughts that I hadn't heard a word the instructor said. Mercifully, when the time came to take the practical part of the test, half of the class took the child sized mannequins and the other half of the class had the adult sized mannequins. I had worked on the adult mannequins before and made sure that I got one of them now. Once we began performing CPR on the dummies my fears and my memories subsided and I did what I needed to do to pass the course.

When I walked out of the room that afternoon, I felt very strong. I thanked God for the strength he had given me, and I was proud of myself for accepting that strength and for using it to help me.

Shortly after I had started my training for Head Start, Doug and I learned that his surgery had been successful!

Doug was outside working when I told him the news. We were so thankful and felt so very blessed to be given another chance at parenthood, and we had a difficult time hiding our excitement from the girls. Not wanting to set the girls up for disappointment, we made the decision not to tell Allison and Kate about having a new brother or sister until we had heard the baby's heartbeat.

We did make one concession and agreed to tell my parents about my pregnancy. I had always told my mom and dad everything, so figured that even if the worst happened and we lost the baby, I would want them to know about it. They were very happy for us, and I think we were all relieved to have a new baby to look forward to.

As all of these changes were taking place in our lives, we received an invitation from the ODN to attend a tree planting ceremony for loved ones who had given the gift of life through organ donation. We were asked to send in a photo of Nick to be included in a slide presentation. We were also asked if we would be speakers at the presentation. We would speak on behalf of donor families, and others would be asked to speak on behalf of recipient families.

Doug wasn't comfortable with the idea of being a speaker, and I wasn't sure I wanted to speak on a topic that was so personal and emotional for me. I thought of Nick, though, and how his story deserved to be told. Speaking at the remembrance ceremony would be a chance for me to tell people who Nick was, how he had helped people, and how we had found comfort through the whole organ donor process. I called the ODN office and told them that I would speak. As I hung up the phone

I hoped that I had made the right decision. I started thinking through things that I wanted to say, and the more that I thought about it, the more confident I became that I had made the right decision.

About a week after talking with the ODN about the remembrance ceremony, I got another call from their office. Expecting to be given additional information concerning the agenda for the night, I was taken by surprise to hear Julie say that she was calling with the update information that I had requested, and she regretted to inform me that she had some bad news. She assured me that the heart and kidney recipients were doing well, but she had also been informed that Nick's liver and bowel recipient had passed away a short time ago. She had no details to give us concerning the date or cause of death.

I felt my loose sense of control disintegrate at her words. There was silence on the other end of the line as Julie let me think about what she had just said. I couldn't believe what I had heard and found it difficult to speak. Julie finally broke the silence by saying that she was sorry to be the bearer of sad news and that if I didn't think I wanted to speak at the remembrance ceremony the following week that was fine.

I wanted to cry, not only for the little girl's loss, but also because so much of what I had made myself believe in had just been shattered. I had put Nick up on a hero's pedestal and had attributed him with Godlike qualities. I had this whole scenario in my mind that allowed me to feel "okay." I was beginning to realize that what I had designed in my mind was nothing but a big sham. I would always think of Nick as a hero and his gifts of life would always be just that, gifts of life, but this small child, his recipient, was still gone.

I know a lot of my confusion came from not knowing the boundary between Nick and God. When I prayed, did I talk to Nick or God? When I asked for signs that Nick was okay, did they come from Nick or God? When I wanted guidance or approval did I ask it from Nick or God? Both were divine and I loved both dearly and I wanted to do right by both. But did I expect Nick to play God? Was I denying God my complete trust and faith by praying to Nick instead of for Nick?

As all of these uncertainties swarmed through my head, I was sure of one thing and that was that I was not going to be able to speak at the ceremony. I felt as though I were letting Nick down by not telling his story, but I had some soul searching to do for myself before I could honor him the way that he deserved to be honored. Julie said she would ask another family to speak and asked if I would like to speak at some other point in time. I appreciated her understanding and told her that I would be honored to be a part of the program in the future. Instead of working on my remembrance speech that night, I sat down and worked on what I wanted to say in the sympathy card that I would be sending to the recipient family.

I worked for an hour or more at the computer trying to put my feelings into words for the child's family. I began my letter with: "I had hoped never to have to write this letter to your family." I ended my letter by saying that I hoped they would still keep contact with us.

Completely drained, I went in and sat down on the couch. The lamp was on low and the girls were in bed. I sat there in quiet, but not necessarily in peace. The little girl's face looked down at me from its place on top of the entertainment center. Nick's picture was a couple of inches away and between the two was a Willow Tree Angel entitled "The Angel of Protection." In my heart I knew that she had been protected in life and would continue to be protected in death. I pictured her with Nick in Heaven, running hand in hand, their hair blowing and great big smiles lighting up their beautiful faces. I could feel peace for her and for Nick, but the thought that haunted me was for Allison, Kate, and the life growing inside of me. I was painfully aware that no matter how hard I prayed, the answer to my prayers would not always be "yes." Nick and this child were proof of that. Nick was the only one of my children that I would never have to worry about.

Although I didn't end up speaking at the ODN remembrance ceremony, we did decide to attend. Since the main event of the ceremony was the planting of a tree in honor of those who had given the gift of life through organ donation, families were asked to bring a paper leaf decorated for their loved one. We had colored Nick's leaf red, and I had glued a picture of him in its center. Around Nick's picture were stickers representing some of the things that Nick had loved: A ball, truck, tools, baseball cap, bucket and shovel, and a tractor.

When we entered the reception room at Hawkeye Community College in Waterloo, we were greeted by staff from the Iowa Donor Network. They showed us the "tree" where we could hang Nick's leaf and then introduced us to some of the people who we had talked with on the phone at the ODN but whom we had never actually met.

Later, a light supper was served and then we were seated in an auditorium for the program. There were several speakers, and all of them had compelling and moving stories to tell. Some of the speakers were in the medical profession, some were with the ODN, some were donor families, and others were organ recipients. It was the recipients who had me hanging onto their every word. As each one spoke, they cried with genuine gratitude for the tremendous life saving gifts they had been given.

The final speaker was an older gentleman who had received a liver transplant. There wasn't a dry eye in the room as he thanked donor families and donors as well. He thanked all of us who had donated as though we had been his donor family. He thanked us for giving him the chance to walk his daughter down the aisle and to spend precious time playing with his grandchildren. He cried with heartfelt thanks and let us feel his love for the person who had lost his life, thereby giving him his. Hearing how these recipient's lives had been improved and saved, I felt honored, proud and blessed to have been given the chance to be a part of such a miraculous process.

When the program had concluded, we walked across the campus to the tree planting. Families that wanted to participate were invited, one by one, to help dig the hole for the tree. Doug, the girls and I each took a turn with the shovel along with the others.

When the tree was at last planted, we were all given helium balloons with lights inside of them, and as one big group, we let them go; one final tribute to our loved ones. It was a strange feeling for me to be standing amidst so many others who were going through loss, but also the experience of organ donation. Eavesdropping on conversations, I heard some families talking about the contact they had had with their recipients. Others were saying how they didn't choose to have contact at all. I felt a little cheated that we had established a good relationship with our recipient family, but that we would never be able to see it through to the final phase, a meeting.

As the balloons disappeared into the evening sky, people started to walk back to the college for refreshments before going home. As we turned to follow, I looked up and saw the liver recipient who had spoken so eloquently at the ceremony. He was standing not far from us and was engaged in conversation with another man. I felt compelled. I had almost an urgent need to speak with him.

I told Doug I would be right back, and without waiting for a reply, walked over to where the two men were standing. They were very kind as they stopped their conversation to look at me, a complete and total stranger, who had just interrupted them. I looked at the man and apologized for intruding. I told him that we were about to leave, and that I wanted to speak with him before we did. I hadn't planned what I wanted to say to him, so fumbled out that we had donated our two-year-old son's organs and that the little girl who had received his liver had just passed away. I choked out the last of my words, but instead of looking at me as if I were some overemotional, distraught woman, he looked at me like he really cared about me and what I was saying.

I told him that I had needed to hear what he said in his speech; about how deeply thankful he was to his donor. I had needed to hear that his life had been renewed, but in his zest for life, he had never forgotten the one who had given it back to him. We spoke for several minutes, and when I excused myself to leave, I gave him a hug. I would never be able to hug the little one that Nick had helped, and he would never be able to hug the one who had helped him. Giving him a hug seemed like the right thing to do.

I think I left the remembrance ceremony that night feeling that, although Nick's young recipient had died, her transplant had given her a year of independent living from the machines and the doctors that had been her existence before the surgery. She had been given a chance at a normal, healthy life, and Nick had given her that chance. Although we hadn't been told the cause of the child's death, we did know from her mother's letters that her last days on this earth had been good ones. We would not have the opportunity to watch her grow through the years, but we did have the opportunity to try and help her, and we had taken it. Despite the outcome, we could and would always find peace and comfort in knowing that we had made the right choice.

We did not hear from the little girl's family after her passing, but in early September we received a letter from the ODN stating that Nicholas' heart recipient (parents) were asking to have their name and address released to us. We were completely shocked by the request as we hadn't had any prior contact with the family. The letters that I had written had gone unanswered and we had resigned ourselves to the possibility that this family may not choose to make contact with us at all. Now all of a sudden, they had requested release of information. We were thrilled.

The letter continued by listing several issues for us to consider before making the decision to proceed making further contact:

Once contact is established the loss of anonymity could have unpredictable results, including contact that you might not be able to control.

The recipient could be curious and want to know about the person who had died.

Some recipients might feel guilty for surviving and communication could make those feelings worse. In some cases, if the organ failed to function well, the recipient could feel that they've let you down.

Be aware that there could be differences in backgrounds, beliefs and values.

Enclosed with the letter was a consent and release form. Doug and I didn't hesitate to sign the form, not imagining any circumstances where we could have unwelcome contact with the family whose baby had been given Nick's heart. We mailed the form and, with unimaginable anticipation, began the agonizing process of waiting for a response.

Our response came surprisingly fast. An envelope containing two letters arrived from the ODN four days after we had mailed our consent form. The first letter was just to inform us that both consent and release forms had been received and that the recipient family's information had been sent to us so that we could make the first contact when we were ready.

It took all of the willpower I had to not just throw the letter down and get right to the name of Nick's heart recipient on the sheet underneath. In my mind I saw us meeting the precious little girl who had received Nick's heart. I saw us meeting in some wide open, outside location. The day would be warm and sunny, and we would step out of our vehicles and make eye contact. The mother would be holding her baby and we would run into one another's arms. The baby would let me hold her and I would cry as I felt her little heart beating strong inside her chest. With a deep and steadying breath I laid down the top letter and at long last allowed myself to read the name on the bottom sheet.

Dear Doug and Erin,

The individual who received Nicholas' heart is a young girl by the name of Brianna. Brianna's address and phone number are…

Her name was Brianna and she lived in Tennessee. My heart soared with joyful anticipation for what I hoped was to come.

We received Brianna's and her family's names and address on September 21. The following night I sat down to write Jeff and Deborah, Brianna's parents. It was Sept. 22, the first year anniversary of Nick's accident. It seemed right somehow that on a day of great sadness, we were given a new beginning of sorts. I turned my grief into hope that our healing could only flourish with the contact between our family and Brianna's.

I decided to write a letter to Brianna and her family rather than call them on the phone. I had an easier time putting my thoughts down on paper than I did speaking them. I thought it best to keep this initial correspondence brief rather than give the family more information than they were ready for. My objective was simply to let them know that we were open to any questions that they had about us and about Nick.

I mailed my letter to Jeff, Deborah and Brianna on September 23 and on October 2, while visiting with Doug's mom and Uncle Gene, who had come for a visit, we got a call. We were sitting at the kitchen table when the phone rang. I picked up the receiver and had to struggle to understand the man on the other end of the line. When I finally got past the thick southern accent, it dawned on me who the man was. I began trembling instantly and started waving frantically for Doug to go get on the other phone. He looked slightly irritated with me for interrupting his conversation until he figured out what I was trying to convey to him. He sprinted to the other phone and we had our first conversation with the family whose lives had become entwined with ours through our children. By the time we hung up the phones, I felt like a tremendous weight had been lifted from my shoulders. Doug and I met back in the kitchen and filled Marlene and Gene in on the gist of our conversation.

It had taken Doug and me a while to get used to Jeff and Deborah's accents, and I think we faked our way through some things they said, but all in all, it was the contact that we had been waiting for. Jeff and Deborah had thanked us repeatedly for our decision that had saved their daughter, and told us of how critical the timing had become for Brianna. If Nick's heart had not become available when it had, Brianna would not have survived.

They told us how the transplant surgery itself had been a miracle. Because Brianna's three-month-old heart had been enlarged, Nick's two-year-old heart had been the perfect size for her. The surgery itself had taken a fraction of the time because Nick's heart lined up in all the right places in the space left by Brianna's heart. As a result of the good match, there hadn't been as much trauma involved for Brianna as there would have been in most other heart transplant surgeries. The swelling in her chest had been minimal and her recovery had been relatively quick.

We learned that Brianna's development had only been slightly delayed by her health issues. At 16 months old, she was close to walking independently, and was saying several words. We were told that she was quite spunky and had no trouble fending for herself against her two older brothers. It made us smile to hear of Brianna's feistiness, because feisty was healthy, and healthy was what we had been praying to hear.

We discussed hopes of meeting, and it was mentioned that Brianna would be celebrating her second birthday the beginning of June. Mentally I was thinking that we would be having a brand new baby right about that time, but said that, if it was at all possible, we would be there. We agreed to send pictures and to keep in touch, and they agreed to give Brianna a great big hug from us.

October brought with it the beginning of my three month ordeal with the Head Start program in Story City. It was the hardest job I had ever taken on and the days, weeks and months flew by quickly. By Christmas time I was ready for Pam to return to school. Being half-way through my pregnancy, I was ready to turn my attention to other things, such as the completion of the new bathroom and bedroom we decided we needed, and the completion of my book.

Also in October, Doug and I found out that we were having a baby girl. My initial reaction to hearing that we were having a third daughter was sadness. It wasn't that I wanted a boy to replace Nick, but I thought I wanted a little boy to wear Nick's clothes and play with Nick's toys. I wanted Doug to have a son to hunt and fish with. By the time we left the doctor's office, my disappointment was gone. It was replaced by excitement for the healthy baby that we were going to have.

On her due date, April 28, 2003, Megan Grace Hulshizer came into the world. As I was giving birth, I held one of Nick's burpies in my hand, and looked at a picture of Allie, Kate and Nick that was sitting on the bedside table. I felt no fear, only peace as our fourth child was born. When the big sisters came to see their baby for the first time, I knew without a doubt that there was a big brother right there with them.

Lying in my hospital bed with our new baby sleeping in my arms, I felt blessed, complete, and content. Our family had come full circle; losing a child, but then being granted the awesome blessing of bringing another child into the world. As I closed my eyes to go to sleep I prayed: "Dear God, thank you so much for all that you've given us. Watch over us and keep us save from harm, violence and illness. And please, please don't let me lose what I already have. Amen."

Epilogue

On the morning of June 7, 2003, we woke up in a hotel room in Goodletsville, Tennessee. I was nervous and anxious and was pacing the floor in front of the mirror. Having given birth to an 8 lb. 8 oz. baby six weeks earlier, I hadn't been able to squeeze myself into many of my pre-pregnancy clothes. We were hundreds of miles from home, about to meet Nick's heart recipient and family, and I was having serious doubts about the clothes that taunted me from the suitcase.

Completely frustrated with myself, I combined the pants from one outfit with the top from another outfit, looked at myself in the floor-length mirror one last time, shook my head with despair, and sat down to try and nurse the baby one last time before we went to the lobby for our "meeting." Megan, of course, wouldn't be interested in a meal until we were in a position where I couldn't feed her, so I handed her off to Doug, and started fiddling with Kate's hair…again.

By the time the phone rang my nerves were stretched thin. Doug picked up the cell phone and began saying words like, "Oh, don't worry about it," and "We understand." I bored holes into the back of his head as he spoke, trying to deduce from his voice and words what exactly was going on. When he hung up the phone, he turned and looked at me and gave me a knowing sigh. They were running late and wouldn't be to the hotel for another half an hour. Normally I would have taken the news in stride. Running late was an everyday event for us, but today…! I really thought I was going to have a stroke or massive heart attack from the way my heart was beating inside my chest.

With the strictness of a drill sergeant, I had the girls sit down on the bed and ordered them to "Watch TV, and for goodness sake, don't touch your hair!" I decided to try and feed the baby again and again she wasn't interested. After fifteen, long agonizing minutes had passed, we decided to head down to the lobby for what felt like the culminating event of a lifelong quest.

The lobby was quite lovely as I tried to force myself to remember all of the details of this moment (and moreover to keep myself from passing out). We knew that Jeff and Deborah drove a Jeep from a previous conversation that we had had, so each time a vehicle drove by we strained to see what kind it was, and each time the car was not a Jeep, I'd try to remember to breath.

When the phone rang again, Doug and I assumed that we must have missed them pulling in and they were calling to tell us they were at the hotel. But they weren't at the hotel, they were calling to say that they were still running late and would be leaving their house shortly. I tried to picture what they must have been going through, too. They had three children to get ready for presentation, plus, should we go back to their house, they would probably want to have the house ready as well. I could completely understand their need for additional time, but, as it was nearing 11:00AM, I was dying!

I sat down on an overstuffed sofa in the lobby, after deciding that the pacing wasn't doing me any good, and tried again to focus on the room we were sitting in. They did have a great fireplace. I looked over at the receptionist and hoped that she didn't know we were from Iowa. The last thing I wanted to do was give the impression that Iowans were a bunch of blithering idiots.

At long last Doug and I saw a Jeep pass by the hotel entrance. We didn't know if Jeff and Deborah had a "going to the beach" Jeep or a "taking the kids to school" Jeep. The Jeep that had just passed the lobby window and pulled into the parking lot was the latter kind. It made sense to us that it was more practical for family use. And it was!

Doug and I positioned ourselves between the front desk and the front door on the off chance that we had correctly identified our recipient's vehicle. When the family who walked in moments later fit the description of the family we were expecting, we knew that we had assumed correctly. The expectancy in our eyes was mirrored in the eyes of the family before us. I could see that they were looking us over to see if we fit the description that they knew. They were at a slight advantage, given that I had sent them pictures, so they had an idea already of what we looked like. But we were seeing them for the first time.

From the moment recognition was confirmed, it was as if some invisible force pulled us together. Like in my dream, Deborah came through the door carrying Brianna, and for a moment, my eyes were only for the blond haired, blue eyed little girl in her arms. As Deborah and Brianna drew nearer, I snapped out of the spell I had momentarily slipped into, the spell where I was comparing two blond haired, blue eyed two-year-olds.

Deborah kept walking towards me until the three of us were caught up in a warm and welcome embrace. We held each other tightly and silently wept with tears of overwhelming gratitude for one another. Somewhere behind me, Doug and Jeff were shaking hands, and our children looked on, not entirely aware of the magnitude of the situation they were witnessing.

The next day and a half we spent getting acquainted with one another's families. We were able to attend Brianna's second birthday party, held in the reception room of a church just down the road from their home. There we were able to meet Brianna's extended family. We were welcomed with loving arms by all in attendance and got to see first hand how much she is loved by her family. When I wanted to cry tears of sadness for the loss of our son, I was able to look around me at the joy and gratitude in the faces of those celebrating a birthday that they had feared may never come. I was able to turn my tears of sadness into tears of thanksgiving that we had played a part in such a grand and heavenly scheme.

On our final night in Goodletsville, as we were standing in the driveway saying our good-byes, Jeff asked if he could send back some things for Nick; things he wanted for us to put next to Nick's stone at the cemetery. We humbly agreed and moments later Jeff reappeared from their home with a white, plastic bag. He told us he hadn't been sure he should give us these things, but when he showed the items to us, we thought they were absolutely perfect.

From out of the sack, Jeff handed Doug a child's toy rescue vehicle, a firefighter action figure and a small plastic firefighter's helmet. Jeff had told us of his love for firefighting, and we had talked extensively about his many years serving as a volunteer firefighter. Doug and I deeply appreciated these tokens of respect and honor that came straight from Jeff's heart to our son. We promised to put them on Nick's stone as soon as we got home.

We were still standing outside in the driveway as the sun completed its descent and the sky turned black around us. Each time Doug and I said that we should leave, one of us would think of just one more thing that needed to be said. Our three children were already buckled in the van, exhausted from the long day that we had had. Jeff and Deborah's son, Codey, had passed out on his bed in the house and Brianna was asleep in her mother's arms. The only child still standing with us was Jeff and Deborah's oldest son, Conner.

When we made the final decision that we really should go, I put my hand lightly on Brianna's back as a final farewell gesture. I had hoped to feel the strong but steady beat of her heart as she slept. I was given something even better. "Do you want to hold her?" Deborah asked me. "Yes, I would," I whispered.

It warred in my mind to have such strong emotions and attachments to a child that I barely knew. I held Brianna tightly, rocking her ever-so-slightly back and forth. The knowledge that I was holding the precious little soul whose body allowed our son's heart to keep on beating, was immensely powerful. As I held Brianna and felt the familiar weight of her sleeping body in my arms, I was acutely aware of the bond that she and Nick shared; a bond that we had chosen to represent in the birthday gift that we had given Brianna for her birthday. As I held her, around her neck she wore a small, heart-shaped locket. The image of an angel was etched on the front of the locket, and on the inside was a tiny little picture of a very small boy with a very large heart.

As we had promised, when we got home, we took Jeff's gifts to the cemetery for Nick. We placed the memorials under Nick's name on our family headstone and took a picture of them. We planned to send the picture to Jeff, so he would know that we had honored his wishes. Seeing the firefighter memorabilia next to Nick's name brought back a memory of the firefighter who had been the first on the scene the night Nick had his accident. I remembered Jeff telling us how hard it was for firefighters to lose someone they were desperately trying to save. I thought of how dedicated the EMS personnel had been when they had tried to resuscitate Nick. Even though almost a year had gone by, I was saddened by the idea that the firefighters and paramedics might have felt they had failed. When we got back home from the cemetery, I sat down and wrote a letter to the individuals who had responded to our call for help the night that Nick drowned:

Dear Ray, Karen, James and Robert,

I am writing in regards to a call you responded to on September 22, 2001. When our two-year-old son, Nicholas, fell in a garden pond, you were there to try and bring him back to us. Despite all efforts, Nicholas was declared brain dead at the University of Iowa hospital five days later. I am writing because, even though Nick did not survive the accident, three others are still alive because of all you did for Nick. Because of the care he was given, we were able to donate his organs. One of the recipients is the little girl in the enclosed photo. She received Nick's heart at the age of three months. We recently were able to meet her and helped her celebrate her second birthday. Her father, incidentally, is a volunteer firefighter.

So from all of us, thank you and God bless you for the work you do.

Doug, Erin, Allison, Kate and Megan

We know that life is not easy; that it is filled with pain, peril and heartache. But we shouldn't forget that it is also filled with love, beauty, and opportunity. My fervent hope is to always feel the love, see the beauty, and take advantage of the opportunities, because we never know when the pain, peril, and heartache are going to come crashing, without warning, into our lives.

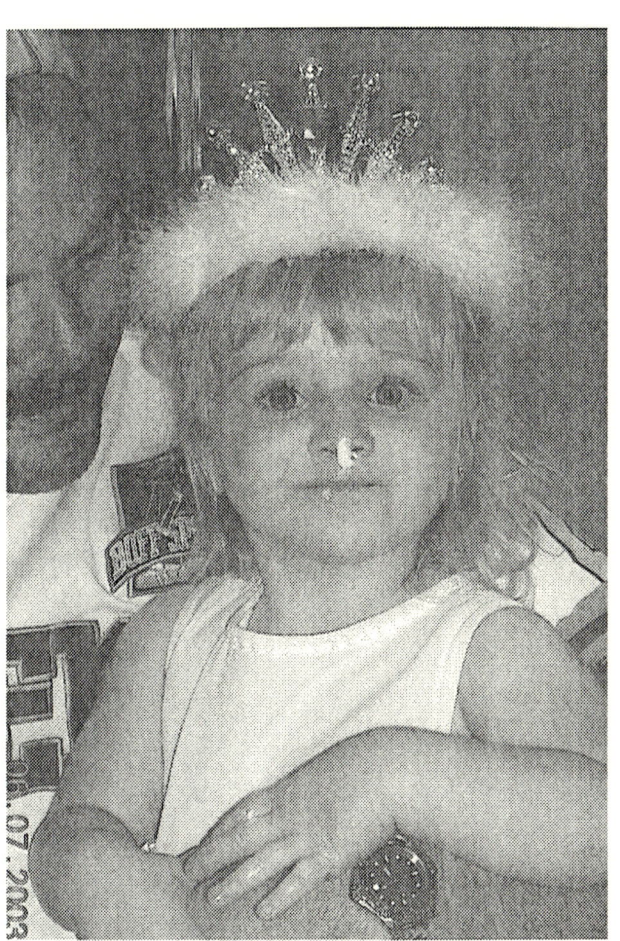

Printed in the United States
40035LVS00001B/337-450